U
MAY
B

THE
ONLY BIBLE
SOMEBODY READS

R U LEGIBLE?

U
MAY
B

THE
ONLY BIBLE
SOMEBODY READS

R U LEGIBLE?

MATTHEW MAHER

ACKNOWLEDGEMENTS

—I humbly give credit where ALL credit is due—

FIRST AND FOREMOST, to my Lord and Savior Jesus Christ, whereas, apart from Him I can do nothing; and only Christ can make something out of the nothing that I am.

I am grateful to Mrs. Cherri Olsen for her professional editing and writing skills.

To my mother for her spiritual encouragement throughout this journey and for training me up in the way I should go (Proverbs 22:6). Mom, you know your role and influence in this book, and honor is always yours.

And to my fellow inmates—friends of the Gospel and even enemies of the Gospel—for without your eyes, I would have never seen the concept of this book come alive. Thank you for presenting me with the opportunity to be the only Bible somebody may read and for proving how dynamic transformation can be triggered by godly influence.

I remain nothing, and ALL the glory, honor, and praise goes to God who has given me the ability and integrity to write out the triumphs and tragedies of being "read."

In honor of Hort Kap and his family.

CONTENTS

Every section contains: a LEGIBLE application of the law;
Four creative illustrations of the law;
And an ILLEGIBLE violation of the law.

*Each chapter is designed to infuse you with insight, that U
MAY B the influence of the law and the inspiration of the Bible.*

biblical influence is rhetorical

*The truest measure of influence is not how much you know
intellectually, but how well you show what you know persuasively.*

biblical influence is supernatural

*Surrendering to the grip of grace will hold you up to a higher
standard of influence.*

biblical influence is motivational

*Catalyst impact isn't compounded by you; it's simplified by
you.*

FOREWORD

By John "Little John" Paladino

"Standing at 6 feet, 2 inches, and weighing 330 pounds, mob enforcer towers over guards as he is brought into the federal court room. John 'Little John' Paladino, a mob enforcer for the Genovese crime family ..."

This was the front page of just one of the papers I read. I scanned the article, then read it through line for line. I smirked at how crazy it all sounded on paper: *Organized crime ... Gambling ... Extortion ... Arsons ... Victims ... Guns ... Money laundering ...*

I've read a lot in my life. Police reports about how I've committed this crime or that crime. Hospital reports about the condition of my victims from my overzealous collecting tactics, along with more front-page articles than I'd care to admit. But one thing I've read the most are the faces and eyes of men who knew I had stepped out of the shadows to collect in blood a debt owed. Those shocked and ghosted expressions were their autobiographies written unaware.

I've read things in black and white; I've read between the lines; I've read poker faces; and I've read the face of fear. The more I think about it, the closer I come to the conclusion that I've read more outside of paper than any written words scribbled or jotted down onto any parchment.

I've had to rely on my innate ability to read men. Their desires. Their covetousness. Their lusts, hate, rage, fear, submissions. Their games and lies. Their stupidities. And in between all of that, their few truths. So when I read a man, I attempted to search his soul by allowing him to reveal it to me with my imposing demeanor. And all the while hoping to read his truth and see where his faith lay—even when faith was misunderstood by me and far from godly. I guess you could say that I did judge a book by its cover—the cover that often was coming undone.

I've stared men down, face to face, and read their insecurities. I've even glared down the barrel of a gun at the terror-stricken victims and read their fright. I've read the pain on the faces of family and friends, as I've been sentenced to periods of time in prison that would break a weaker man.

And now with hindsight 20/20, I wonder what all of my victims, family members, and friends have read on my face and in my eyes? But that was all before I finally read someone that read me back and assessed me accurately. HE, Jesus Christ, truly saw into my soul—and that is why I gave HIM my life. And in a setting that I had seen before, yet this time I saw something more.

I spent almost half my life in the setting of prison and was quick to persecute "people of faith" no matter their race, creed or color. They were always quick reads for me; but then again, none were ever willing to open up to me. Or maybe I wasn't willing to open up to them. Nonetheless, their book covers were never appealing, and I recall being turned off by their contrary actions from the book that they claimed to live by: the Bible.

You see, I never picked up a Bible for that reason nor considered faith in anything except in myself. Until 2011. Until my fourth prison bid. Until I began to read a 28-year-old Bible that opened my eyes to Jesus Christ.

During this same time period, I received a brand-new Bible with my name and verse inscribed onto the leather-bound cover. It was a very beautiful Bible that was given to me as a gift for my birthday by a friend.

But truth be told, the Bible I enjoyed even more than this nice leather-bound one was the 28-year-old one that I happened upon in prison. I found it when I first arrived at Mid-State Correctional Facility, N.J., on March 15, 2011. Although I wasn't much into reading the Bible, the words of this Bible literally came alive and spoke out to me through parables and teachings that I never knew existed in the Bible.

At first, as I read it, I paid attention to the words of this older Bible because of its soothing voice and interesting message. I also had it with me every day (and still do), learning from it and asking it to reveal its message to me because I had doubts and lacked understanding. Truthfully, I didn't understand a thing in other Bibles, including my new one.

But this 28-year-old Bible never failed to unveil and spill out the truths—the tidings and good news of Jesus Christ. My new leather-bound Bible was nice, but at times it was hard for me to understand the message. All of the *thou*s and *shalt*s, the fire and brimstone. I felt confused, guilty, and worse—unsure.

But my 28-year-old Bible put it in laymen's terms that brought Jesus and His teachings to a whole new light. I studied my 28-year-old Bible every day. I learned from it the most outside of Bible-study time, by following the examples it gave me—such as being more loving and more filled with mercy.

If it weren't for God placing this 28-year-old Bible on the bunk next to mine, I doubt I'd be saved today. So at the tender age of 46, after years of reading police reports, hospital records, newspapers, and people—often for dishonorable reasons—it has been my privilege and pleasure to read my 28-year-old

Bible's countenance, seeing that what he projected was real faith. What I have read in him can only be explained as the "living word"—the Word alive in human form. He is a doer of the Word.

Although the "Good Book" was always within reach, it wasn't needed because what I read in my 28-year-old Bible was clear enough to reach me. And that Bible, through his legible example of the Word, showed a mob enforcer how to read the Son of Man; how to accept Jesus the Christ as my Lord and Savior; and how to humbly be the Bible that somebody else may read.

If you haven't figured it out yet, I'm proud to tell you that Matthew Maher is my 28-year-old Bible and the very reason that I now desire to be a good read myself. I just may be the only Bible somebody else may read. With Christ's strength alone, I am now a servant of Father God, not the godfather.

John "Little John" Paladino
servus servorum Dei
2012

PREFACE

It's so PROFOUNDLY SIMPLE, it's simply profound! And it has been a statement that my mother gently pounded into me when I was growing up. I heard it, but I would not always heed it. In fact, it is this very "I" test that I failed to examine, believing myself to have 20/20 vision in my own mind's eye. I was blind then. I knew the Bible—but it's not about reading it, but *being* it.

Say what you want, but it took tragedy for me to go from an intellectual Christian to an experiential Christian. A Bible reader to a Bible heeder. And since this transformation and realization, I have learned that it is impossible to be effective and influential for Christ when your proclamation of faith does not line up with the "I" chart that's portrayed and displayed.

"Matthew," my mother would say before I left the house, "you may be the only Bible somebody reads!"

Essentially, she was telling me that people are always reading you! Always watching. Analyzing. Is what they see *legible*? Can a person's faith be observed outside of church, Bible study, and prayer groups by those who may never consider faith otherwise? Or the contrary: Are you *illegible*? Is confusion and hypocrisy the language of your book? Are you a bad read?

I lived my life in the babel state of confusion, but no more! I am now determined to reveal the Bible and its truths in my new state of creation. New in Christ because Christ has made me brand-new in *character*, *conduct*, and *conversation*; and I'm committed to this script and the renewal of it!

Therefore, my mother's words have penetrated more than these prison walls; they have been a constant reminder to me in this current chapter of my life to "write" clearly into others' lives that:

U MAY B
THE ONLY BIBLE
SOMEBODY READS

I have found her statement in my current placement to be more than precise, like the exacting slice of a scalpel wielded in surgery. Not many read the Bible in this place, so I knew early on how crucial it was for me to "save face" for the sake of God's grace! Because of the raw and real substance behind this arrested conclusion, I know rightly from here on out that I will only be successful when I follow the example of the ONE who was radically liberated even though He was incarcerated by flesh Himself.

Jesus, the walking and talking Bible, was being read continually by His peers; and by the freedom He displayed, the wisdom He conveyed, and the grace and truth He portrayed, many found themselves captivated by His pages and set free by the same. His "book" is not bound by stitches and glue, but abounds in liberty and makes the reader brand-new. So we must read Him within that we may walk and talk Him without. As if my momma already knew back then that we would become a paperless society today, she would be quick to remind you too, saying, "You may be the only Bible somebody reads."

INTRODUCTION

"You may be the only Bible somebody reads."

Now you've heard it said to you, but only God can write it in you, like a Master Surgeon using His scalpel to take you from just a surface consumption of the Word on paper to a visible demonstration of the Word in person. And to be visible is to make the law of liberty visual. But first you must look intensively into the perfect law of liberty as if you are looking at an eye chart. And how your "I" sees responsively all depends on the vision of your heart. Is your vision blurry or do you see with clarity? Because how you view the Bible will truly dictate how you are reviewed outside of the Bible. As you will see throughout this book, I was a man with double vision. When you have one foot in the world and one foot in the Word, the result is divided living. I was also a man who had Christ, but I failed to let Christ have me. So at various times in my past I was whatever the crowd needed me to be. But now with hindsight 20/20 and foresight directed by eternity, it is my intention in this book to help you with your biblical reflection and to positively instigate your character's projection.

The Bible declares beautifully that Christ is "the brightness of God's glory and the express image of His person" (Hebrews 1:3). And perfectly, the Greek word translated *express image* is *charakter*—and means "the engraved or stamped mark, image or representation." Vibrantly therefore, Christ is the exact representation of God's nature and exactly who we should project in our nature. His "express image" needs to be our character expressed—character stamp—which brings me back to the image we reflect and how it all depends on what we're looking into and if we are keeping the eyes of our example in check. Thus, an "I" check-up is exactly what the doctor ordered. So, let's do so by looking into the law together. First with the Old Testament (OT) prescription. Then with the New Testament (NT) "script" renewal.

LOOKING INTO THE LAW

The purpose of "looking into the law"—from the OT meaning to the NT meaning—is to stimulate biblical education in order to expand your reading comprehension as it pertains to wielding godly influence:

The Bible declares in the Old Testament, *"This Book of the Law shall not depart from your mouth, but you shall meditate in it day and night, that you may observe to do according to all that is written in it. For then you will make your way prosperous, and then you will have good success"* (Joshua 1:8).

> The Hebrew word *torah* translated "Law" in the text above, signifies primarily direction, teaching, and instruction. It is derived from the verb *yarah*, "to project, point out," and hence to point out or teach. The law of God is that which points out or indicates His will to man. It is not an arbitrary rule, still less is it a subjective impulse; it is rather to be regarded as a course of guidance from above. Seen against the background of the verb *yarah*, it becomes clear that *torah* is much more than law or a set of rules. *Torah* is not restriction or hindrance, but instead the means whereby one can reach a goal or ideal (Strongs Concordance #8451).

One goal of looking into *"this Book of the Law"* is to project spiritual prosperity and good success, which means "to act wisely." Your example of godly living ought to be a beacon of instruction and direction. Therefore, by placing your "I" into *"this Book of the Law"* to be taught by the Spirit of truth, you'll begin to embody the spirit of the law, which is appropriating spirit and truth.

The Bible declares in the New Testament, *"But be doers of the word, and not hearers only, deceiving yourselves. For if anyone is a hearer of the word and not a doer, he is like a man observing his natural face in a mirror; for he observes himself, goes away, and immediately forgets what kind of man he was. But he who looks into the perfect law of liberty and continues in it, and is not a forgetful hearer but a doer of the word, this one will be blessed in what he does"* (James 1: 22-25).

> The Greek word *nomos,* translated "law" in the text above, signifying of a force or influence impelling to action. "The law of liberty" is a term comprehensive of all the Scriptures, not a "law" of compulsion enforced from without, but meeting with ready obedience through the desire and delight of the renewed being who is subject to it; into it he looks, and in its teachings he delights; he is "under law (*ennomos,* "in law," implying union and subjection) to Christ." (Strongs Concordance #3551).

Looking into the law is an action word stressing obedience. The law of liberty will influence you and then influence others through you. Therefore, by placing your "I" into *"the perfect law of liberty,"* you will reflect your spiritual face in the mirror—Christ—that others will be able to mirror to find Christ. That's "doing the Word."

MARRYING THE LAWS

The Old is the New concealed. The New is the Old revealed. The sum of the whole is Christ revered. Likewise, **U MAY B** an old Christian or **U MAY B** a new Christian, but both spectrums alike need renewed vision. As stated earlier, how you view the

Bible will truly dictate how you are reviewed outside of the Bible. The Psalmist rightly expresses, *"Open my eyes, that I may see wondrous things from Your law"* (Psalm 119:18). And I add, *"that* **I MAY B** *wondrous things from Your law!"* Thus, in this catalytic book, you become the spiritual reaction to the theme's substance of conviction. I challenge you to interactively read this book knowing you too will be read outside the pages. An individual may have no clue what is printed between Genesis and Revelation, but the truth is: The genesis of your conviction dictates the revelation (unveiling) of your gospel. The message you're putting forth. Apply the laws in this book and you'll be a legible presentation of Christ. Violate the laws and you'll be an illegible contradiction of Christ. The choice is yours.

HIS WORD = ONE WORD

Friend, knowing that **U MAY B THE ONLY BIBLE SOME-BODY READS** is reduced to one word: Influence. The law of the Lord is perfect influence and that which converts the soul. *"The law of the Lord is perfect, converting the soul"* (Psalm 19:7a). Since Christ is influence, then Christ in you makes all the difference. And when looking into the eyes of Christ through His Word, your "I" will begin to see with the eyes of Christ at this world. Those around you—at home, in school, at work, in prison, wherever—need to catch what you have. Your biblical example ought to be contagious. The word *influence* comes from the Italian word *influenza*, which means "an acute and highly contagious virus disease marked by fevers, aches, pains, and other respiratory symptoms." No, I'm not saying that influence is coughing or breathing on somebody, but it's allowing God to breathe on somebody through you. Just as the flu can be infectious, so should your conduct and countenance be contagious. Now that's true influence, and that is why the purest form of biblical example is influence through inspiration.

Don't know where to start? Start by placing your "I" into the *U MAY B Challenge* (see *Appendix*) and turning it into an **I MAY**

B charge. The more you get into Scripture, the more Scripture will get into you—backed by God's breath: *"All Scripture is given by inspiration of God, and is profitable for doctrine, for reproof, for correction, for instruction in righteousness, that the man of God may be complete, thoroughly equipped for ever good work"* (II Timothy 3:16). The "inspiration of God" (Gr. Theopneustos) comes from the Greek word, which means, "God breathes," from *theos* (God) and *pneo* (to breathe). Thus, throughout this book my purpose is to induce influence, which must be leveraged by "Bible-breathed" proof. Inspiration! And since **U MAY B THE ONLY BIBLE SOMEBODY READS,** then like Braille, in order for others to read you, they must feel you. The Holy Spirit in you. Without the Spirit of truth navigating you through the pages of this book, as well as educating you through the challenges of life, inspiration and influence will not be possible.

THE COMPLEX MADE SIMPLE

As you look into the laws presented in this book, it is my desire to inspire INFLUENCE through "express imagery" as well as personal transparency. The design of the book consists of 11 parts that appropriate 11 unique laws of biblical influence, where the LEGIBLE and ILLEGIBLE chapters in each section are personal examples that contrast proper *application of the law* with the improper opposite— *the violation of the law.* The chapters sandwiched between LEGIBLE and ILLEGIBLE in each part are *the illustration of the law* that uses creative metaphorical images to stamp Christ's character, conduct, and conversation into the pages of your life. Each of these respective chapters includes "Bible-breathed" endorsement (INSPIRATION) and concludes with an **I MAY B** reminder (CHARACTER STAMP) that summarizes the imagery expressed with an expressed image. Major in these laws and allow the law of the Lord to be your Teacher. *"Blessed are the undefiled in the way, who walk in the law of the Lord"* (Psalm 119:1).

VISION RESTORED

Finally, as you "look into the laws" and begin to appropriate the concepts and precepts illustrated in this book, understand that the process doesn't stop there; now it's up to you to "lawyer" written example into weighted execution by taking the INFLUENCE from the pages of this book and becoming the Bible that causes a nonbeliever to take another look. Friend, I am writing "the vision" (Habakkuk 2:3) and by doing so, I'm asking you to partner with me in the mission. **I MAY B** one person and **U MAY B** one person, but together we may be one movement.

It starts with me where I am, and it gains momentum with you where you are. As author Simon Sinek said, "The visionary must light a flame. Those who choose to follow its light must work to keep it burning."

I concur, yet I remain but a spark that desires God's glory to set ablaze revival and renewal in this land. We can do it because it all begins by taking a spiritual stand. The Bible breathes, *"If My people who are called by My name will humble themselves and pray and seek My face, and turn from their wicked ways, then I will hear from heaven, and will forgive their sin and heal their land"* (II Chronicles 7:14)

IF WE ARE GOD'S PEOPLE, it's time to wear His name without shame. Too many people wonder, "What happened to the God of the Bible?" And that is why we must be the Bible that shows the people our God. Committing the Bible to memory is respectable. But committing the Bible to life, that is wisdom. So before you read on, let us check our *vision*. Instead of covering one eye with your hand, cover your own life with prayer. If you truly desire to be read by your peers the way the Living Word inspires it, pray with me now that we may make sure the "I" chart that we put out is a legible representation of the Word of God within:

O Lord, please allow me to be more than just an "e-reader" of Your Word, but consistently a "doer of the Word." Father, I ask You to please write the TRUTH in the "nook" of my heart for I desire it to "kindle" a flame that shows others the WAY to you. O Lord, make my LIFE like our "paperless society" that shows off Your Son by the way I live and love, and not just by the book I hold. Father, please remind me that I may be the only "I-pad" that somebody might ever see; and by the content I display on my "screen," let it be pleasing and acceptable as the "apple" of Your eye. Amen.

CHARACTER STAMP:
I MAY B the Bible.
That's not spirituality.
That's reality.
Accountable. Presentable. Readable.

PART I

---

the law of HIS WITNESS

"The truest measure of influence is not how much you know intellectually, but how well you show what you know persuasively."

appropriating the law:

Biblical influence is rhetorical. And only you can be an eye witness for your "I." You better believe that this "I" will be tested, so are you ready to be a witness of God's grace and mercy in your life? Communicating this law is having an awareness of your own testimony and being ready to share it when necessary. Sometimes when the questions about our faith arise, we are not properly prepared to answer accordingly. But by knowing this law, you already know that it is your eye that will be put to the test—therefore, what have you seen God do in your life? Be ready and willing to persuasively show what it is the Lord has done, as you help someone else's gaze on the Son become clear.
U MAY B A WITNESS!

Be ready to testify with clarity and consistency.

~seeing the law is being the law~

LEGIBLE

-application of the law-

"[A]nd you shall be witnesses to Me ..." (Acts 1:8).

When projecting the law of HIS WITNESS, we are to be a legible representation of the *character*, *conversation*, and *conduct* of Jesus Christ.

I've heard it explained that a leader's best ally is his own example. But going deeper than "my own example," I must recognize that I am not my own witness of what I did or can do. And I'm not even someone else's witness of what that person did or can do. I am to be HIS WITNESS, telling of the things that only God did and can do. It's not complicated! In fact, consider these words, which are the most simplistic, yet intrinsic example for us to understand what it is to communicate the law of HIS WITNESS: *"He answered and said, 'Whether He is a sinner or not I do not know. One thing I know: that though I was blind, now I see'" (John 9:25).*

In John 9, the man who was once blind did nothing but state the obvious as his testimony—*"I was blind, but now I see."* He was being a witness to God's healing power in his life, and that is certainly the clearest Bible somebody will ever read—our testimony. The one thing the once blind man knew was the only thing that he needed to know. And that's what he showed, by simply telling of new sight contrasted with his blind plight.

Wait! Surely to be legible as HIS WITNESS we must be profound and eloquent in our testimony, right? Wrong! Like the

> INFLUENCE:
> *He can never be at a loss for*
> *words who has believed on the*
> *Word.*
> JEROME, 347-420 A.D.

blind man, all that we have to do to successfully witness for Christ is to soundly state the irrefutable and personal facts of what it is God has done for us—how He has *saved* us, *changed* us, and *delivered* us. Being HIS WITNESS is not an argument or debate. It is allowing somebody to read the Bible through your testimony or example. Sharing your verbal testimony is intentional. It requires you to purposely communicate God's glory in your life—whether it pertains to what He's brought you through or what He's kept you from. When you are committed to applying the law of HIS WITNESS to your life, like the man whose vision was restored, you can be sure God will always provide an audience for this influence.

In the year of 2006, I was a junior in college at Temple University. I was a student-athlete and had just returned to school after a very surreal winter break, during which we had buried my oldest brother, John. He was 28, and I was 21 at the time. His sudden death on December 15, 2005, caught everyone who was attached to John completely off guard. Just four months prior to this tragedy, John's first and only child was born, a precious daughter they named Alivia Maher. The coming Christmas season was to be the first of many categories. A baby's first. A father's first. A first for my other two brothers and me as uncles. And a first for our parents as grandparents. Alivia's life was the highlight of joy for all of us that Christmas, especially her proud daddy. However, none of us would have ever imagined life being such a great magnifier of death. Her birth. John's death. A course in funeral etiquette and a lesson on grief were the educational experiences of my Christmas college break.

A month after John's death I returned to my duties as an undergrad, while also maintaining my responsibilities as an athlete. I did not slip behind in either area of college life, but I knew that I needed to go deeper than just returning to campus and carrying on with "business as usual." It would have been too easy to simply go through the motions after such a tragedy, but the Christ in me was rising up after death.

I was a member and regular attendee of the Fellowship of Christian Athletes (FCA) on my campus. We met weekly for Bible study and testimony-sharing. It was a great time of camaraderie among the various sports teams at Temple University.

> INFLUENCE:
> *The nature of human beings is to be inactive unless influenced by some affections: love or hatred, desire, hope, fear, etc. Those affections are the "spring of action," the things that set us moving in our lives, that move us to engage in activities.*
> JONATHAN EDWARDS, 1703-1758.

I was an outspoken participant because of my background in faith, having grown up in a Christian home, but up until this point I wasn't sure if my words were legible to the group. I needed to present myself differently—not just *knowing* it, but *showing* it.

There would have been no better opportunity to communicate the law of HIS WITNESS to my peers as an example of God's grace and recipient of His peace than the testimony of triumph I had to offer, following the tragedy that had recently struck my family. Telling someone how the Bible may work in his or her life is a whole lot different than sharing with someone how the Bible has worked in one's own life. And when I say "the Bible," I mean "the Word." And when I say "the Word," I mean Jesus Christ—*"And the Word became flesh"* (John 1:14a). That's the law of HIS WITNESS, allowing the Word to be heard through our flesh.

At an FCA meeting and in the presence of my peers, I decided to share with them this testimony about what my family and I had just been through—the cessation of life—and how God had seen us through the celebration of death. With tear-filled eyes and a shaking voice, I pushed my way through this testimony. Telling everyone that God is still good even though the outcome from our perspective isn't. I was real as real could be not because I was taught the subject at hand—mourning loss 101—but because the Teacher had held me by the hand and took me through the subject. There was nothing eloquent or clever about the presentation; I told them plainly and in a straightforward manner about a grace and peace that buffered and guarded me during this extremely difficult time. I told them about how my family used the funeral as a platform to evangelize the gospel of Jesus Christ, regardless of the grievous setting. We used Jesus' birth to celebrate my brother John's death—and eternal life. Was it easy? No. Was it worth it? Absolutely. This testimony before my peers told them of the "one thing I knew" and that was how death tried to blind us, but God gave us spiritual sight to see life through it all. There was no need for a Bible verse to correlate with my words because my countenance and conduct spoke the language fluently. My words and tears were HIS WITNESS—enough to convince my peers that God truly comforts and sustains in times of need, and in times of loss.

> INFLUENCE:
> *You may not think so at first, but tragedy brings clarity to your witness. It grabs the attention of your audience and provides the opportunity to testify to God's comfort. Practical Insight: God comforts us not to make us comfortable, but to make us a capable comforter.*
> MATTHEW MAHER, 1984-

On that particular day and at that exact moment, I was the very Bible that my peers were able to read. I was legible. And all because the spoken word emanated from an inner source of strength. I didn't know what I was even going to say that day to the group, but being the only Bible somebody may read knows that God will give you His words to be HIS WIT-NESS at the precise time for His glory. And that's the eloquence within the law of HIS WITNESS, where it's not how much you know intellectually, but how well you show what you know persuasively.

ATHLETE

-illustration of the law-

To communicate the law of HIS WITNESS, be an athlete. Be *disciplined*, *determined*, and *deployable*.

All athletes know that being disciplined involves the body and mind, but this is Christian athletics and must always include the spirit. Just as an athlete trains to be at the apex of physical performance, so must a believer train inwardly for spiritual excellence to show outwardly. Your ability to exercise discipline and self-control will be the first introduction of your Bible to any potential onlookers.

An athlete carefully monitors what he places in his body; so, too, must you—physically, mentally, and spiritually. Nutrients and protein-rich foods fuel the athlete's growth and maintain his stamina. He is attentive in his consumption and diligent in his exercise. An athlete knows he is only as good as his intake—"you are what you eat." Likewise, being the only Bible somebody may read requires you to be disciplined in your diet.

> INSPIRATION:
> *But I discipline my body and bring it into subjection, lest, when I have preached to others, I myself should become disqualified.*
> I CORINTHIANS 9:27

Do others see you eating the Word, working it out in prayer or flexing your faith muscle? I'm not talking about a pharisaical display—that is, a rigid observance of religious rituals without real faith or devotion. I'm talking about a consistent discipline, which is a legible read that clearly shows Christ in your heart.

Furthermore, an athlete must be determined. He must push himself beyond comfort. He must be willing to endure through pain. Before the race or game even begins, he throws the quit option away and focuses in on the prize. The win. For believers, here is the pressure remover and endurance fueler: The victory is already won. The Christian athlete begins his race at the finish line, in victory lane. He merely determines himself to follow in the footsteps of Christ.

In other words, being read as an athlete requires you to be seen as one who never gives up. One who will keep pushing beyond the comfort zone, knowing that with resistance comes the building of strength. Mind, body, and spirit must be unified to be a legible Bible; and like the athlete, each component must be prepared for competition and determined to be victorious.

> INSPIRATION:
> *Everyone who competes in the games goes into strict training. They do it to get a crown that will not last, but we do it to get a crown that will last forever. Therefore I do not run like someone running aimlessly; I do not fight like a boxer beating the air.*
> I CORINTHIANS 9:25-26 (NIV)

Finally, an efficient and effective athlete must be deployable. With all the athletic ability in the world, if you don't play nice with your teammates, you cannot champion any purpose nor serve a winning cause. The coach cannot use you. Like a deployable athlete, being the only Bible somebody may read is being teachable and usable. It's about following the coach's instructions and heeding his rebukes.

Without a servant's attitude of ready obedience to go where the coach asks you to go or do what the coach tells you to do, you will have benched yourself on the sidelines. The audience watches those in the fray and overlooks those who don't play; so to be legible, one must be in the game, with knowledge of the game plan.

Be legible. Be an athlete.
Be disciplined. Be determined. Be deployable.
Be the Bible!

CHARACTER STAMP:

I MAY B an athlete. The athletic mindset is the competitive mindset; and with performance often comes an audience. He who is disciplined in practice is habitually qualified for the game. Thus, it is your discipline that separates you from your peers. The law requires you to practice self-control in mind, body, and spirit when in private so that your reason of use inspires you to live with reason when in public.
I MAY B an athlete.

Remind yourself that the separation comes in the preparation.

SOLDIER

-illustration of the law-

To communicate the law of HIS WITNESS, be a soldier. Be *prepared*, *purposed*, and *perceptive*.

The dynamics that make up an athlete may also be found in a soldier. However, the soldier is not playing a game—he is fighting with his life on the line. There are certain elements that a soldier embodies that make him comparable to a Christian. Sometimes, it is these very qualities to which a nonbeliever is attracted because they tend to naturally engender respect. With the wise application of Scripture verses, and not bashing heads with the Bible, a soldier can wield his weapon with power and precision accuracy. This requires the delicate handling of Scripture—treating it more like a sniper's rifle, and not reckless machine-gun spray. In honor of the rules of engagement, preparation for battle is necessary not only for one's own good, but also for the good of others. It is better to be a sharpshooter with Scripture than to have a blasting approach. Nobody responds to carelessness. "People don't care how much you know until they know how much you care" (Theodore Roosevelt).

In fact, being the only Bible that somebody may read is a responsibility that involves accountability. As a soldier for Christ—His walking warrior and talking word—you must be engaged in the battlefield of life and prepared, with biblical acumen, to have a word in season for the weary or the wayward. For example, most of the Proverbs and Psalms are appropriate tools that can be pulled out of your arsenal to help encourage

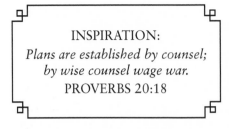

INSPIRATION:
*Plans are established by counsel;
by wise counsel wage war.*
PROVERBS 20:18

or heal a wounded comrade. It is beneficial to memorize such Scriptures because many listeners are turned off right away by the mere mention of the Bible; but when you know the Word and use it conversationally, the recipient does not even know—at first—he has been impacted by the Word of God.

Furthermore, like a soldier, a Christian has purpose. As the war for souls is constant, will you be the Bible that wins a soul? Are you purposed in your heart to ensure your example, though bold, is not cold? It's about having your mind—your aim, your goals, your focus—set on things above. On an actual battlefield, it is not always easy to know who your enemy is; hence, the soldier must be on constant alert. With proper preparation and planning comes the ability to carry out your purpose. And the purpose is simple for a soldier: Be honorable at all costs. Even when suffering, a soldier does so successfully.

INSPIRATION:
You therefore must endure hardship as a good soldier of Jesus Christ. No one engaged in warfare entangles himself with the affairs of this life, that he may please him who enlisted him as a soldier.
II TIMOTHY 2:3-4

Being read as a soldier requires you to fight through the blitz of warfare in this life. It's a given: sudden bombings of tragedy; gunfire hardships; the loss of a loved one; the diagnosis of a terminal illness; and a host of other afflictions. Yet the soldier goes through his trials with an unparalleled peace that relies fully on the commander-in-chief. For the Christian soldier, that is the peace of God, administered by his Commander-in-Chief.

Suffering successfully with purpose at heart is what will catch the eyes of those who are watching. Why? Because they will see you boldly, yet humbly, handle afflictions that felled others as casualties of war.

Finally, an efficient and effective soldier is perceptive. With all the military knowledge and training in the world, if you have no vision, you cannot properly assess your battlefield. Your situation. Your life. Like a perceptive soldier, being the only Bible that somebody may read is being able to see clearly by relying on your faith, not on your sight. Discernment is not just observance. To be perceptive, one must line up his eyesight with his insight.

Discernment is the ability to judge well in order to gain direction or understanding. Without discernment, you will put out the wrong message, and those reading you will be confused at what your intentions are with them. You must know when to press forward and when to retreat, when to speak up and when to shut up. The radar is always on; so to be legible, one must be aware of his surroundings—knowing that others are attempting to read and interpret him as well.

> INSPIRATION:
> *Put on the whole armor of God,*
> *that you may be able to stand*
> *against the wiles of the devil.*
> EPHESIANS 6:11, see
> verses 11-20

Be legible. Be a soldier.
Be prepared. Be purposed. Be perceptive.
Be the Bible!

CHARACTER STAMP:

I MAY B a soldier. A soldier is obedient and responsive to commands with singleness of purpose. The most effective soldier is one whose soul is infused with boldness and balance. He must be ready to "go" on command and "halt" on demand. Therefore, understanding the law is recognizing that you must obey God at all costs, leaving the consequences to Him (Dr. Charles Stanley). Looking into the Word is holding yourself to a higher calling than the world.
I MAY B a soldier.

Serve with unquestioning obedience and leave the outcome up to God.

FARMER

-illustration of the law-

To communicate the law of HIS WITNESS, be a farmer. Be *hardworking, holding,* and *hopeful.*

Every productive farmer knows that he is only going to get out of his land exactly what he puts in it. A farmer is responsible for his own produce; and by the hard work of his hand, comes the fruit of the land. Without hard work, there can be no appreciable accomplishment. Therefore, to be the only Bible that somebody may read, you must be willing to partner up with hard work and realize that you are always in the process of sowing your land. Your land is the environment in which you live—the community that consists of the people, places, and things with which you come into contact, and includes those people, places, and things that your "seed" will eventually touch. Yes, our scattered seeds have far-reaching effects.

An essential biblical principle is expressed with an agricultural analogy: *"Whatever a man sows, that he will also reap."* A farmer knows that if he plants corn, he can expect corn—and not wheat—to grow. In order for the farmer to expect with certainty a wheat crop to spring forth, then he must plant wheat—and not corn or soybeans or alfalfa. Likewise, when we plant our seeds as Christians, we have the assurance that what we sow is exactly what we will grow. The planting of seeds can best be explained by how we live out, walk out, and speak out God's Word. And those seeds that are not planted can never grow—in other words, God cannot bless what you do not do.

> **INSPIRATION:**
>
> *Do not be deceived, God is not mocked; for whatever a man sows, that he will also reap. For he who sows to the flesh will of the flesh reap corruption, but he who sows to the Spirit will of the Spirit reap everlasting life. And let us not grow weary while doing good, for in due season we shall reap if we do not lose heart.*
>
> GALATIANS 6:7-9

Our hard work, then, is comprised of the attitude and the actions that are cultivated through our many life experiences. The more land that is plowed and the more seeds that are sown the more likely that the farmer can expect produce and gain in due season. However, before the season of reaping comes the season of holding.

To be holding as a Christian is to know that our patience must precede us. Indeed, we must be the embodiment of patience. We may not see our seeds growing, but that does not mean there is nothing going on beneath the soil. After a farmer completes the hard work of planting, he must wait. Waiting is a prerequisite to the harvest. It is by God's grace alone that there is a harvest; you can be sure that He is the One responsible for growth. Thus, like the farmer, we wait with patient expectation—that's the hopeful component.

If the hard work is invested and the season of holding with patience is understood, hope is the absolute expectation of forthcoming fruit. Hope is what makes the process well worth it; without hope, without hard work, and without holding in patience, a farmer is nothing more than a gambler. As walking, talking Bibles, we are not foolish gamblers—we are people of faith. Like the farmer, it is our faith that produces the substance: *"Now*

> **INSPIRATION:**
>
> *Therefore be patient, brethren, until the coming of the Lord. See how the farmer waits for the precious fruit of the earth, waiting patiently for it until it receives the early and latter rain.*
>
> JAMES 5:7

faith is the substance of things hoped for, the evidence of things not seen" (Hebrews 11:1).

Essentially, onlookers will know you are different by your faith—which is not just an attitude, but an application. They may understand the importance of hard work, and they may even understand the

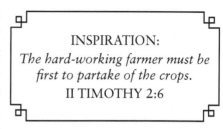

INSPIRATION:
The hard-working farmer must be first to partake of the crops.
II TIMOTHY 2:6

concept of holding in patience. But one thing that makes your example attractive, appealing, and intriguing to watchful eyes is the hopefulness apparent in your demeanor.

Finally, a farmer is always on guard for weeds. If left unchecked, the weeds will choke the growth of the good seed. In the life of a Christian, weeds can be temptations that distract us; if left unchecked, they could choke our growth and destroy the harvest. Temptations can come in many forms, including other people. Therefore, as a farmer, one must learn how to deal with the weeds. If the weeds are other people, the *Golden Rule* is necessary as your environmentally-friendly weed controller—more than a "weed killer," it is a seed healer. If you treat everyone as a potential seed, a believer, for the Kingdom of God, then you can be the very Bible that somebody may otherwise never read. Now that's legible farming.

Be legible. Be a farmer.
Be hard-working. Be holding. Be hopeful.

Be the Bible!

CHARACTER STAMP:

I MAY B a farmer. A farmer does not watch his crop in anxiety. A farmer waits on his crop with expectancy. A farmer labors patiently and strenuously, and by the fruit of his yield, his neighbors take him seriously. Essentially, it is patience that produces a mature work in you, and it also promotes God's work in you for others to see. When you think you can't wait with expectancy, like a farmer, just think WAIT! And this is what you can expect to see: a harvest of perseverance and the reaping of calm assurance in yourself.
I MAY B a farmer.

Labor with love for your neighbor, and you will certainly reap good favor.

WITNESS

-illustration of the law-

To communicate the law of HIS WITNESS, be a witness. Be *truthful, trustworthy,* and *tender.*

In the Court of Christianity, what is your role? When tried, what is revealed? If you were to be prosecuted right now for your faith, would they have enough evidence against you to convict you of being a Christian? Would anyone know that you are HIS WITNESS?

Being the only Bible somebody may read is knowing that you are constantly on trial. But in this court procession, you are to have only one role. The witness. And as the witness, one must be expected to "show and tell" the truth, the whole truth, and nothing but the truth—certainly with the help of God. Sounds easy, doesn't it?

However, we complicate matters by taking on other roles. Why, for instance, do we sometimes act as the prosecutor—accusing, assuming, and speculating? Or how about when we make ourselves out to be the judge—condemning, rendering judgments, and meting out punishments? We even think we need to be lawyers for God—debating, justifying, and arguing for the

> INSPIRATION:
> *He who believes in the Son of God has the witness in himself [. . .] and this is the testimony; that God has given us eternal life, and this life is in His Son. He who has the Son has life [. . .].*
> I JOHN 5:10-12

truth. But he who justifies does not convince. The truth needs no help. When will we comprehend the simple fact that as a truth-teller, we are to do nothing but testify as Christ's witness—showing and telling about the things He has done in our lives? We testify not only by our words, as the evidence is made even clearer by our deeds.

The witness who takes the stand must be trustworthy and tender. He who calls a witness does so because he knows the truth will flow freely from that witness. With that being said, I have to ask this: Does God see you as a credible witness? Can He put you on display, on the witness stand? What the witness is going to say and what the witness will portray are both extremely important to the court's case. Because the jury is always watching, your truth-telling and compelling truth must always be done in love. Truth without love is brutality, and love without truth is hypocrisy.

> INSPIRATION:
> *A faithful witness does not lie, but a false witness will utter lies.*
> PROVERBS 14:5

Fundamentally, being legible in the Court of Christianity is knowing the truth intimately. It's about allowing the truth to set you free and making your stance on the stand not contrived nor forced. As I stated previously, the jurors are always watching, and it is their trust that you must aim to gain. Nonbelievers will never know what makes a Christian any different if we do not set ourselves apart by the truth. When the Truth is embodied, Christ-like *character, conduct,* and *conversation* is not embellished. Therefore, being the truth is accepting the Truth—and even having the Truth trust you. *"Jesus said to him, 'I am the way, the truth, and the life. No one comes to the Father except through Me'"* (John 14:6).

You CAN handle the Truth—because **U MAY B THE ONLY BIBLE SOMEBODY READS,** and Judgment Day will come to all men. Will you be the very witness that helps save a soul? Is your stance on the stand of life legible? Are you HIS WITNESS or His hindrance? Can the Truth trust you? God wants to put His Word in you to good use—honor that conviction!

> INSPIRATION:
> *Then Jesus said to those Jews who believed Him, "If you abide in My word, you are my disciples indeed. And you shall know the truth, and the truth shall make you free."*
> JOHN 8:31-32

Be legible. Be a witness.
Be truthful. Be trustworthy. Be tender.
Be the Bible!

CHARACTER STAMP:

I MAY B a witness. An effective and efficient witness testifies with concise integrity. He takes the stand and already knows that his truth is not swayed by judge, jury or judicial system. A witness rightly divides the word of truth, which means "to cut straight" (Gr orthotomeo), as one who is not concerned with useless debate. When you examine your own "I" and handle your own witness with integrity, you are aware that others' ears can become their eyes—meaning, what they hear you say will be how they see your faith.
I MAY B a witness.

Remember that the integrity of your soul is found on your lips.

ILLEGIBLE

-violation of the law-

"He who speaks truth declares righteousness, but a false witness, deceit" (Proverbs 12:17).

I may have begun with a time when I was legible as HIS WITNESS, but there were plenty of times when I was illegible. It wasn't just that I was unreadable; I was, in fact, ungovernable. Clearly out of control! Thus, it is fitting that I share such examples with you that you may learn from my bad witness and do better. The thought of being so illegible makes me ill. And it should, as it is those past shames that drive me deeper in His name.

You see, this imprisonment has pulled so much out of me that I did not even know was in me; and when I think about my past illegibility, it is very sad that I sold myself—and my Lord—short all of those years. Complacency will keep you in a comfortable mold, keeping HIS WITNESS hidden inside without you even knowing where He resides. Purposely, that is why God allowed adversity to break me out of that mold, shake me out of that complacent hold that He may get me to behold HIS WITNESS and shine like gold. Being a legible witness is gold for the soul.

INFLUENCE:

Man's greatness and wretchedness are so evident that the true religion must necessarily teach us that there is in man some great principle of greatness and some great principle of wretchedness. It must also account for such amazing contradictions.

BLAISE PASCAL, 1623-1662

Now I find myself thinking literally in every situation, "What Would Jesus Do?" (Charles Sheldon). Remember the WWJD movement of the 1990s? At the time, I did not really grasp the significance that those initials could have on every aspect of my life. *I wore the bracelet*, not letting the reminder embroidered on *the bracelet wear me*.

This is where I showed myself as a false witness—opposite of what I was wearing on my wrist. Perhaps those present and watching me in the situation would not have known what I claimed to represent had it not been for the bracelet, which makes you think about the symbols we wear that declare our faith—jewelry that feature the cross, clothing emblazoned with Bible verses, tattoos depicting religious art or slogans. Yet, is our *character, conduct*, and *conversation* lining up with those witnesses?

But I was wearing the bracelet! And because I was not spending time in the Word with Jesus, I had no clue what the effective and attractive answer to that question would have looked like in this incident of which I am about to tell you. WHAT WOULD JESUS DO?

Back then I knew what the initials stood for, of course, but if I did not truly know what Jesus would do, how could I answer, "What Would Jesus Do?" And because I didn't know how to clearly apply the law of HIS WITNESS, I put out the wrong text by wearing this bracelet and acting contrary to the bracelet's reminder.

I was a false witness by my actions on this cold evening, late in the fall, at Temple University. It was my freshman year, and our dormitory's fire alarm went off just before midnight. This had occurred

INFLUENCE:
Christ our Lord, who, because of His great love,became what we are so that He might bring us to what He Himself is.
IRENAEUS, 115-202 A.D.

previously, so I already knew the procedure, which required us to be lined up outside the dorm before the fire department could come clear the alarm. Mind you, the entire dorm—hundreds of students—were scattered in controlled chaos at a safe distance from the building. I took my position, wearing my Adidas winter jacket, near the main door so I could be the first one back in. I hate the cold!

We knew it was a fire drill, but little did I know that I was about to start my own fire—far from a drill. At this time, I was speaking to a young woman, Amber, who lived on the first floor in my dorm. When Amber saw me, she came over and tucked herself in my big winter coat. The jacket was roomy and warm, and she was cold. *How could I refuse her?*

As Amber snuggled up beside me in my jacket, we were spotted by Kelly and a group of her friends. Kelly and I both lived on the fourth floor and had become good friends. Now, I knew that both Amber and Kelly liked me, but I had not been forthright in disclosing to Kelly about my new friend Amber from the first floor. When Kelly and her friends saw me with Amber, it quickly became apparent that they were appalled and disgusted because they had caught me with another girl wrapped up in my jacket. Heck, if they had asked me at the time, I would have had room for Kelly to snuggle up as well.

Nonetheless, I knew that I had been discovered, too, but I found no fault in what I was doing because I had shown interest in Kelly but had not given her any indications of exclusivity. And this is where the WWJD bracelet and my testimony as a Christian were caught in the middle of my false witness.

Soon, from among the circle of friends surrounding Kelly came one of her guy friends to confront me about this situation. As he approached me, I knew it wasn't going to end favorably for anybody. I took off my jacket to keep Amber warm and out of the way, ironically putting the WWJD bracelet on full display. He chose some harsh words for me, letting me know how messed up it was that I had led Kelly on and embarrassed her. He also let me know that it wasn't going down like that. I was going to offer him some space in my big warm jacket as well, but instead I answered him with an even tone. "What does this got to do with you, and I suggest you stay out of this."

Like a rattlesnake, my vibrating response was a warning before the strike. I had a reputation as a tough athlete to uphold, right? I mean, in spite of claiming to be a Christian and wearing a WWJD bracelet? Wrong! That testimony and witness for Christ should have been the only reputation and character that I cared to uphold.

So similar to a rattlesnake already engaged, I did strike. I hit this guy because I felt like he was threatening me. In reality, he was looking out for a friend. He was honorable to my despicable. The hard slap caught him off guard—disarming him and dissipating any initial courage he had in approaching me. However, in reducing him, he reduced me even further as he pointed at the bracelet on my wrist. With words that have echoed in my soul ever since, he said, "And you're supposed to be a Christian! That's definitely not what Jesus would do."

He turned and walked away. He was the victor, and I had spoiled everything. I not only lost the outward battle, but I had sabotaged myself and lost the inner war. I knew what the initials meant, but so

> INFLUENCE:
> *True leading leads to true changing. It's getting those who follow you to believe in the path you're blazing; not only through your sweat and tears, but ultimately from the only blood that can cover your peers. Christ is the leader's leader; and if anyone ever desires to lead people in life, it is a must to read Jesus Christ. Without His leading being the legible example that you're bleeding, there is never a trail for others to see. Practical Insight: To find out "What Would Jesus Do," read red—Jesus' words highlighted in the traditional gospels.*
> MATTHEW MAHER, 1984-

did this guy. No matter how much I knew, it didn't matter because that's not what I showed. By my contradictory conduct, I was a false witness. I was illegible.

So, what would Jesus do?

Today, I have come to this answer *out* by learning how to consider this question *in*: in hatred, what Jesus did; in strife, what Jesus did; in suffering, what Jesus did; in accusations, what Jesus did; in betrayal, what Jesus did; in all the trials He faced, what Jesus did.

On that particular day, I violated the law of HIS WITNESS. I now know that when you allow that question to wear you, putting it on in every situation like a shirt, then the response that is pulled out of you will reflect the Jesus that is in you.

"But put on the Lord Jesus Christ, and make no provision for the flesh, to fulfill its lusts" (Romans 13:4).

VISION RESTORED

U MAY B farsighted or you may be nearsighted, but neither will amount to anything if you are not "insighted." You see, without discernment, which is when your eyesight lines up with your insight, you have no sight. Your witness will come in clear when you focus on clearing out the vision of your heart. By flushing out your "I" with the water of the Word, you will begin to see purely in the world. "To the pure all things are pure, but to those who are defiled and unbelieving nothing is pure; but even their mind and conscience are defiled" (Titus 1:15).
Clarity, therefore, is not only sight, but insight.
U MAY B HIS WITNESS!

Never neglect the inch though you can see the mile. Tend to the outlook by taking an honest look within.

PART II

---

the law of HIS INSTRUMENT

"Surrendering to the grip of grace will hold you up to a higher standard of influence."

appropriating the law:

Biblical influence is supernatural. It is your "I" that becomes an instrument when you make your "I" HIS INSTRUMENT. "[I]t is no longer I who live, but Christ lives in me," *Paul writes in Galatians (2:20)—he became an instrument of grace by taking on Jesus' name. Likewise, you must know that as a tool, device or utensil, you can only be useful when you place your "I" into God's hands to be used by Him. Thus, utilizing this law involves instrument-checking by introspection. Ask yourself whose grip is tighter on your life: God's grip or your own grip? You will know by the squeeze, for God's hands always allow you "room to breathe" (one meaning of the Hebrew word for "salvation").*
U MAY B AN INSTRUMENT!

Remember that your output is only as instrumentally eternal as your input.

~seeing the law is being the law~

LEGIBLE

-application of the law-

"And do not present your members as instruments of unrighteousness to sin, but present yourselves to God as being alive from the dead, and your members as instruments of righteousness to God" (Romans 6:13).

When projecting the law of HIS INSTRUMENT, we are to be a legible presentation of the *character, conversation,* and *conduct* of Jesus Christ.

I like to say that the difference between placing your life in God's hands and taking life into your own hands is comparable to the difference between lightning and a lightning bug. Both may radiate light, but let's check the voltage! When we surrender our lives into God's hands and become HIS INSTRUMENTS, we become conduits for His lightning power. High-voltage influence!

He needs us to be His devices, His utensils, and His tools that remain steadfast in His grip of grace, that we may be used to "write" out His purpose, "magnify" His name, and influence the very world around us. Furthermore, I am to utilize the law of HIS INSTRUMENT by allowing God to put forth His hand and use me as an "instrument of righteousness" regardless of the platform or the receptiveness of those around me. Consider these words: *"Then the Lord put forth His hand and touched my mouth, and the Lord said to me: 'Behold, I have put My words in your mouth'" (Jeremiah 1:9).*

In Jeremiah 1, the prophet was to do nothing but speak the words that God wanted to amplify through him. Jeremiah was being an instrument of God's message and was to proclaim exactly what God placed in his heart regardless of his own youth and even the people's stubborn hard-heartedness to the message. Wait! Surely to be legible as HIS INSTRUMENT we must be as strong as a power tool or as charming as an orchestral collaboration, right? Wrong! Like Jeremiah the prophet, I am merely a microphone for God: His words resound through my mouth unaffected by Matthew Maher—my age, my background or anything else about me. You see, being HIS INSTRUMENT requires you to be nothing more than the device God chooses for you to be in that moment. It's about allowing somebody to read the Bible through your surrender to the grip of grace.

> INFLUENCE:
> *Just as a writing-pen or a dart has need of one to employ it, so also does grace have need of believing hearts [. . .] It is God's part to confer grace, but yours to accept and guard it.*
> CYRIL OF JERUSALEM,
> 313-386

In January 2013, while still incarcerated, I had the opportunity to be nothing more than God's microphone. In a videotaped interview with *The Press of Atlantic City*, I was presented with a platform to have my story broadcasted to the public. I have done many interviews as a professional athlete, so I know how easy it is to be assertive, take the microphone into one's own hands, and answer the questions motivated by self-promotion.

And I know how easy it is to spin the message for the media—giving them the generic and secular in order to please or appease. But not on this day, because my desire to inspire was driven by the conviction within me to be legible as the only Bible those present may read.

The reporter was accompanied by the Corrections Officer and the representative from the N.J. Dept. of Corrections.

The two officials were there to make sure I didn't say anything amiss against the institution. For each one present, prison was an extremely alien place. Even a CO typically doesn't have a clue what it's like on the inside of the inside—a place where it is assumed no light dwells and where the default setting of an inmate's outlook is depression.

I knew all of these assumptions, but I had my heart set on a different type of reflection. In fact, I knew that the interview had nothing to do with my voice being accepted, and everything to do with God's voice being projected. So I wanted Him (and those present) to first see my demeanor completely contradict the environment. I greeted the reporter with a joyful, "Thank you kindly for taking the time to come here," thereby "writing out" my inner attitude before he could even write down any of my verbal answers. I then took my seat in the assigned area where he and I were to meet. On the table were his voice recorder and video-recorder, awaiting our dialogue.

The reporter came to interview me almost four years after the tragedy and the reason I was currently in prison. So the fact that the press wanted an interview at this time can only be explained by two words: God's grace. The reporter probably did not know this, but I was not going to allow this interview to go down without letting them all know this. I desired to be HIS INSTRUMENT, making myself the microphone for God's glory, and not forsaking the message for the sake of the platform.

It was right then, at that moment, that there was no better opportunity to utilize the law of HIS INSTRUMENT. The reporter asked many questions, from the

> INFLUENCE:
>
> *When you do receive praise for something you have done, take it indifferently and return it to God. Reflect it back to God, the giver of the gift, the blesser of the action, the aid of the project. Always give God thanks for making you an instrument of His glory for the benefit of others.*
> JEREMY TAYLOR, 1613-1667

tragic night of that fatal accident to my current stay in prison. He asked about my past, my future, and dwelled obviously on my present. Yet, no matter what he asked or how he framed the question, I answered as nothing more than a microphone, magnifying God's grace over my life.

> INFLUENCE:
> *Your depth of heart will determine your length of influence. And with every platform comes great responsibility. Whether one person or one million people, both bodies deserve the same level of passion. Practical Insight: You can impress from afar, but you'll impact up close.*
> MATTHEW MAHER, 1984-

I talked about liberty and peace in spite of confinement. I shared that this platform wasn't about me or my story, but it was about being an instigator of integrity for God's glory—provoking positive change. I gave him biblical answers. I responded legibly and with clarity. I didn't care to use this publicity outlet for the exposure it would offer. No! I wanted to be the only Bible those present in that prison room may ever read. I wanted to be nothing more than a microphone in God's hands. That's what the law of HIS INSTRUMENT is all about, where surrendering to the grip of grace holds you up to a higher standard of influence. Without His grip, there'd be no grace.

PENCIL

-illustration of the law-

To utilize the law of HIS INSTRUMENT, be a pencil. Be *writing*, *wiping*, and *willing*.

Ever thought about being a pencil? Yeah, me neither! Not until prison, not until this was the only permissible instrument given to us inmates for writing purposes. It is only a golf pencil, barely 2 inches long. Yet, it still works. It is still able to write, able to erase, and able to be sharpened. This little No. 2 pencil got me thinking about being just that—a little, insignificant No. 2 pencil. A pencil that writes out exactly what God desires to write out through my life. But one must be willing to be held—and controlled—by another in order to be used as a pencil. Held in God's hand! Controlled by His Holy Spirit!

Being the only Bible that somebody may read is about leaving your mark wherever God leads you. No matter the surface. No matter the conditions. And how fitting is it that it is with lead that the pencil is filled. Thus, in order to be a servant LEADer, one must be filled with Christ to lead by serving. Service is what piques nonbelievers' curiosity. They cannot figure out what would drive someone to compassionately help others, esteeming others over oneself. That is why loving service is where God first begins to write

> INSPIRATION:
> *My heart is overflowing with a good theme; I recite my composition concerning the King;my tongue is the pen of a ready writer.*
> PSALM 45:1

out the Bible's message through you. Your acts of service will leave pencil etchings of love everywhere you go. Those watching don't need to read about love in the Bible to know love. You just need to be the love in the Bible to let them see the love of the Bible.

Just as God wrote out His story (History) for our understanding and His glory, so too must we allow Him to write out our destiny for His manifestation of glory. But not first without a wiping! Forgiveness. You must know that you can erase and correct any mistakes that you've made in your life by asking for and accepting God's forgiveness. Likewise, because you are forgiven, you must forgive. You must be willing to use your eraser to wipe out the sins of others. No judging; no condemning; but setting yourself apart by the blessing of directing others into how they are to wipe away their guilt and shame. Show them how to navigate their own erasers.

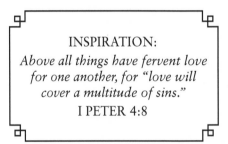

INSPIRATION:
Above all things have fervent love
for one another, for "love will
cover a multitude of sins."
I PETER 4:8

A pencil is only as usable as its sharpness. Therefore, are you able to be sharpened from time to time? Are you willing to suffer successfully through a painful sharpening, knowing that every trial we face is meant to strengthen us and make us better pencils—better writing instruments in His hand? The most important part of us is on the inside, so we consider it joy to face trials—knowing that the testing of our faith will bring the usable inside out!

Consequently, how you handle the "pencil sharpeners" of life is the drastic difference between cursing and cursive. Being the only Bible that somebody may read is like cursive writing—writing out Christ in a Holy Spirit-joining and continuously flowing lifestyle, no matter what you're going through. As the writing brings the symbols of language together to express a legible message, so too will your life express God's messages of love and unity.

If you are not willing to be held and controlled, willing to be "lead," and willing to be used, your pencil will be dull—it may even break in despair. And a pencil with a broken point cannot leave a legible mark. The universe is God's paper; to be legible one must know how to write out the Word by being the Word.

> INSPIRATION:
>
> *Let not mercy and truth forsake you; bind them around your neck, write them on the tablet of your heart, and so find favor and high esteem in the sight of God and man. Trust in the Lord with all your heart, and lean not on your own understanding; in all your ways acknowledge Him, and He shall direct (write out) your paths.*
> PROVERBS 3:3-6, parenthetical emphasis added

Be legible. Be a pencil.
Be writing. Be wiping. Be willing.
Be the Bible!

CHARACTER STAMP:

I MAY B a pencil. A pencil writes with lead and erases with its head. When using this utensil, you know that you can clean up when you mess up. Thus, like a pencil, you must always be consciously aware of how you are led (by grace) and how God holds nothing over your head (by mercy). God forgives. So keep writing (and going) with His lead, and keep accepting His erasing.
I MAY B a pencil.

Keep mercy on your mind and "lead by grace" in your heart.

PIANO

-illustration of the law-

To utilize the law of HIS INSTRUMENT, be a piano. Be *balanced*, *bearing*, and *bridging*.

U MAY B THE ONLY BIBLE SOMEBODY READS, and your *U* is everything that is attached to you! Being an instrument of the Bible is more than your living example—it is the lyrics conveyed through your written example. Letters. E-mails. Text messages. Facebook feed. Twitter tweets. Blog posts. Instagram caption. Our written word outside the Word! How is our character literally being read?

For example, I've turned my word processor in prison into a piano! When each musical note is pushed in balance and melodic order, the song that is produced can be seen with the eyes, caught with the mind, and felt in the heart. It's my way of bridging the distance between my physical presence and my metaphysical presence. It's about how people read us in the abstract when we are not there in the concrete.

Your written words are like music, pushing down the keys on your computer or phone is how you play your tune. Each entry may contain a different groove and dance move, but the cadence remains the same. The balanced rhythm is the consistent expression within that must continuously show without; being the only Bible that somebody may read has to do with everything that you put out. Is what you assign online a representation of Christ?

Here are a few tips, a few key-strokes that may help. First, know that the back-beat of your music sheet is already auto-tuned into place, which means that it's important to recognize God's administering of undeserved grace.

> INSPIRATION:
> *Let your speech (and written messages) always be with grace, seasoned with salt.*
> COLOSSIANS 4:6, parenthetical emphasis added

Subsequently, you won't write your own music with inappropriate text. Don't lose heart when you hit the wrong note or play off-key; just get back in tune with the Word—back to the right music sheet and back to the right beat.

Like a piano, let the "hammers" be the means to reach the strings of hearts as you share the Bible's beautiful music—a message that is beautiful even (perhaps especially) in times of tragedy. Don't babel based on feelings. Post the Bible based on faith. Consider this! It takes about 18 tons of pressure exerted on the stretched strings of the piano to create a beautiful harmony. In the majestic concert grand, the amount of pressure is closer to 30 tons. Pressure produces passion and perseverance.

Essentially, being read as a piano is knowing the difference between black and white. It's knowing that the keys you push create the words that you endorse. Nothing could be more hypocritical than claiming to be in line with the Bible in real life, then putting out online filth in your cyber life. That's building a dangerous bridge that cannot bear weight—neither the weight of scrutiny nor the weight of a

> INSPIRATION:
> *Finally, brethren, whatever things are true, whatever things are noble, whatever things are just, whatever things are pure, whatever things are lovely, whatever things are of good report, if there is any virtue and if there is anything praiseworthy— meditate on (and put out) these things.*
> PHILIPPIANS 4:8, parenthetical emphasis added

heavy load. You create an untrustworthy link, a disaster in the making.

Ultimately, remember that your written output should be like the finest symphony, composed to bless all those who hear.

Be legible. Be a piano.
Be balanced. Be bearing. Be bridging.
Be the Bible!

CHARACTER STAMP:

I MAY B a piano. A piano that plays on its own stands alone; but with the musician on the keys, the piano plays to the audience's needs. It is their ears that the pianist wants to strike with a chord, that the piano's tunes will bring praise back to the musician. In essence, fine-tuning your "I" is knowing that the instrument makes the music, but it is the Musician who makes the instrument.
I MAY B a piano.

Let your work of faith be heard and your Savior's work be seen.

SURGE PROTECTOR

-illustration of the law-

To utilize the law of HIS INSTRUMENT, be a surge protector. Be a *conduit, and let Him do it.*

Understand this fundamental principle first, and everything else in your life will generate "electricity." In order to have any power, or the capability to be any type of legible example, you must be plugged into God. You must continually be connected to His word; or as Jesus described it: *"I am the vine, you are the branches. He who abides in Me, and I in him, bears much fruit; for without Me, you can do nothing"* (John 15:5).

In other words, God's power is like electricity, and we are nothing more than the conduit through which that power flows. As conduits, we allow the Holy Spirit's current to move through us, work through us, and even sustain us. For without Him, we can do nothing!

The world is filled with "electricians"—self-help gurus—who are constantly trying to tell you and sell you the multiple packages that all contain the same theme: willpower. But one thing that cannot be over-looked, and which will be the only Bible that some may read, is the Holy Spirit-power in your life. Even nonbelievers attached to you will see the Bible in you by the way

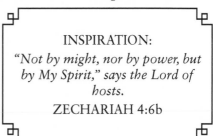

INSPIRATION:
"Not by might, nor by power, but by My Spirit," says the Lord of hosts.
ZECHARIAH 4:6b

you remain stable even through a "blackout," when willpower fails. They will have been able to keep functioning off of your conduit. They will have found comfort based on your comfort—the comfort of the Holy Spirit, who is the Comforter. That's dynamite power!

> INSPIRATION:
> *Blessed be the God and Father of our Lord Jesus Christ, the Father of mercies and God of all comfort, who comforts us in all our tribulation, that we may be able to comfort those who are in any trouble, with the comfort with which we ourselves are comforted by God.*
> II CORINTHIANS 1:3-4

Being a surge protector is about staying plugged into God's outlet, while protecting those who will find themselves plugged into you. How so? Since you are plugged into God's Word, you possess the power that may sustain anything connected to you. When life's raging storms cause (will)power fluctuations and outages, those attached to you (who are attached to God) will be blessed by their connection to you. *"For the unbelieving husband is sanctified by the wife, and the unbelieving wife is sanctified by the husband [...]" (I Corinthians 7:14).*

Furthermore, electricity is dormant unless it has an outlet. So once the power is in, it must be given out. Being the only Bible that somebody may read is about being open to cleansing, conviction, and conversing. Without allowing God's Word to cleanse and convict you, there will be no conversation that leads to conversion. It is only by the Holy Spirit's manifestation and power that faith is produced in others.

In fulfilling your role as a surge protector, you can continually give because you will continually get. You do not have to worry about replenishing yourself or even worry about wasting "electricity." As long as you stay plugged into God as a conduit, then He will faithfully show up in you to show out through you.

Without openness to the Holy Spirit, your own will-power will fail. It will always blow out. But when you respond to life's "blackouts" with a peace and power that is not of this world, nonbelievers will take notice. They will want to "buy in" to your electrical source, because the

> INSPIRATION:
> *And my speech and my preaching were not with persuasive words of human wisdom, but in demonstration of the Sprit and of power, that your faith should not be in the wisdom of men but in the power of God.*
> I CORINTHIANS 2:4-5

storm that blew out their circuits was the same storm that powered your faith.

You may be the only Bible that somebody reads! You may be the only conduit that somebody needs! Stay plugged in!

Be legible. Be a surge protector.
Be a conduit and let Him do it.
Be the Bible!

CHARACTER STAMP:

I MAY B a surge protector. A surge protector is a power holder, but a surge protector cannot hold power unless it is plugged into the source of power. Thus, the outflow is only as strong as the connective inflow. When your "I can do it" mentality turns into a "He can do it" actuality, your "I" becomes a conduit reality. It is your connection in Christ—plugged in— that allows His power to work through you.
I MAY B a surge protector.

Understand the power is not from you, but from the Source into which you are plugged.

THERMOSTAT

-illustration of the law-

To utilize the law of HIS INSTRUMENT, be a thermostat. Be *controlled, consistent,* and *responsive to the climate.*

This may be the most challenging Bible to be, but in order to be HIS INSTRUMENT it is exactly what you must be. Personifying a thermostat is being a Christian who sets the air temperature wherever you go, no matter what is going on. It's about transforming your environment because you are controlled by the right temperament.

It is very easy to be influenced by those around you and even by the circumstances that surround you, but being the only Bible that somebody may read is about being consistent in character, caring in conduct, and clean in conversation—no matter who you're with and where you are. You must bring Christ with you; and by your disposition, you will be one who warms up any place or person. Consider how Jesus hung out with sinners, yet it was He who changed them and not the other way around. He was consistent and controlled, responsive and bold. It is written that *"bad company corrupts good habits,"* but when you are a thermostat, your positive habits change your company.

To be like a thermostat, you must be automatic. Whether the temperature in your life plummets to freezing or soars to boiling by unexpected adversities, you must allow your default faith to click on to carry you on. This healthy setting must be achieved and maintained by being in the Word each day. When you renew your mind's temperature daily, you do not worry about your culture changing you—because you've already made up your mind to change your culture. Additionally, when the tempers of friends or foes are turned against

> INSPIRATION:
> *And do not be conformed to this world, but be transformed by the renewing of your mind, that you may prove what is that good and acceptable and perfect will of God.*
> ROMANS 12:2

you, it is your ability to stay in control that once again sets the climate tone. Your response in the face of hot-tempered or bitterly cold people is what will be read by others. When they read your demeanor, they will be attracted to the finding that you've stayed consistently kind. Remember, this begins in the mind!

Without control over your mind, body, and spirit, you will be like a hot sauna, sweating your way through life, or a freezer frosted over, which keeps you cold in your emotions. You must keep yourself well-insulated in the Word. You control your internal climate, and whatever degree is set within will eventually come out!

U MAY B THE ONLY BIBLE SOMEBODY READS. Thus, taking on the characteristics of a thermostat is allowing God to be your temperature-setter. Sometimes He will require you to be calm, cool, and collected in order to

> INSPIRATION:
> *Whoever has no rule over his own spirit is like a city broken down, without walls.*
> PROVERBS 25:28

provide His peaceable breeze. Other times, He may require you to be the heat that helps melt away someone's frozen countenance. You never know what adjustment to make unless you are controlled by Christ, consistent in the Word, and responsive to the climate.

INSPIRATION:
Set your mind on things above,
not on things on the earth.
COLOSSIANS 3:2

It is a mindset and a heart's attitude. It's a clear forecast even if your environment is downcast. It's being legible by being consistently credible. It's being a transformer, not a conformer. Therefore, are you willing to be a climate and culture changer?

Be legible. Be a thermostat.
Be controlled. Be consistent. Be responsive to the climate.
Be the Bible!

CHARACTER STAMP:

I MAY B a thermostat. A thermostat does not conform to its environment—it transforms its environment. A thermostat dictates the temperature, bringing the degrees of separation into agreement with its regulation. It instrumentally influences cold air with warm care, and it turns heated situations into cool conditions. Therefore, applying this law is setting your mind to the right degree above in order to alter the wrong intensity below.
I MAY B a thermostat.

Recognize that being under the influence of the Word is influential in the world.

ILLEGIBLE

-violation of the law-

"And do not present your members as instruments of unrighteousness to sin" (Romans 6:13a).

I may have begun with a time when I was legible as HIS INSTRUMENT, but there were plenty of times when I was illegible. It wasn't that I was just unreadable; in fact, I was unstable. Clearly double-minded! Thus, it is fitting that I share such examples with you that you may learn from my wrongly applied representation as an instrument and do better.

When ILLegible, I was ILL. Sick. But it is because of these ill experiences from my past that my faith is now well. Such symptoms are the constant reminders of my present health in Christ, and that which keeps me checking my "spiritual temperature" to assure a legible read as I surrender to the grip of grace found in the law of HIS INSTRUMENT.

It is in my here and now that I rely on this personal "thermometer" to examine my own work and to continually check myself to keep myself in check; but I did not always use this instrument properly. Sadly, instead of using it to *"examine yourself as to whether you are in the faith" (II Corinthians 13:5),* I acted like a thermometer by adjusting to whatever

> INFLUENCE:
> God [. . .] has been careful to heal opposites with opposites, that those things which were ruined by pride might be restored by humility.
> JOHN CASSIAN, 360-435

the setting needed me to be. From bar-hopping to church-stopping, and everything in between. I would change based on the degree of the atmosphere that I entered. I was a double-minded man.

Similar to the example I presented in this section's LEGIBLE about doing an interview in prison and being an instigator of integrity, I now want to share with you a time when I said all the right things in a sports interview as a professional soccer player, only to be a blatant ILLEGIBLE example only a few days later—an instigator of tragedy.

I did this radio interview with my older brother Anthony—not only as pro soccer players and teammates for the Philadelphia Kixx, but as members of Athletes in Action. Athletes in Action is a Christian organization of professional athletes who use sports as a platform to share their faith. A few notable AIA members are soccer stand-out Tim Howard and NFL greats Reggie White and Kurt Warner. Now, my brother and I were members, with our very own player cards that featured our pictures and testimonies.

Once again, a microphone was one of the choice instruments used by the reporter visiting our locker room in the legendary Spectrum arena. This historical sports complex was home to the Philadelphia Flyers of the NHL and the 76ers of the NBA. From its opening in 1967 to its closing in 2009, the Spectrum hosted countless events, sporting contests, and musical concerts—from Jimi Hendrix to Pearl Jam and the U.S. figure-skating championships.

I was beyond blessed by God to be where I was; but instead of becoming a microphone to magnify God, I manipulated the microphone to magnify me. I answered in all the right ways about faith and being a Christian as a professional soccer player. I spoke Bible, but was far from living Bible.

I told the radio reporter everything he expected to hear from a well-known athlete who was also a Christian, but little did he know that I was only conforming to the temperature that was required of me in that moment. The problem wasn't my stance in this interview or in life in general; the problem was my failure to consider a fall. *"Pride goes before destruction. And a haughty spirit before a fall" (Proverbs 16:18).*

> INFLUENCE:
>
> *It was my concern from day to day, to say neither more nor less than what the Spirit of truth opened in me, being jealous over myself lest I should say anything to make my testimony look agreeable to that mind in people which is not in pure obedience to the cross of Christ.*
>
> JOHN WOOLMAN, 1720-1772

I was playing with God and showing off, when the Bible was expected to be showed off. Meanwhile, I would do more than enough showing off outside of any church setting, and for worldly reasons. I failed to consider how this vice of pride (and other vices for that matter) led me to being used as the wrong device—*"an instrument of unrighteousness to sin."*

As a result, I was fully responsible for causing the death of an innocent man named Hort Kap in a fatal drunk-driving accident on the Atlantic City Expressway. I became a literal instrument of destruction in my vehicle the night of March 7, 2009, and if I were the only Bible that somebody may have read via that interview or even on my player card, I would have been a completely contradictory and confusing translation. Not "would have been"; I WAS! Believers and nonbelievers alike would have had trouble reading the incoherent message that I recklessly put out. It was far from Bible and full of babel.

I still feel this illegibility in my heart—not because I am not forgiven, but because I think about how many times I was a stumbling block to those watching me closely due to my faith stance. They would have seen me embody the wrong characteristics of a thermometer—an instrument that goes with the mercury flow determined by outward conditions. I was whatever the crowd needed me to be. Foolishly, I was a conformer. But no more!

> INFLUENCE:
> *The humble heart is the brave heart. And a brave heart does not compromise conviction no matter the circumstances. Practical Insight: Success can sabotage your humility and integrity; reflect often to keep yourself in check.*
> MATTHEW MAHER, 1984-

Immediately after this tragedy, Anthony contacted the radio reporter and told him about what I had done. We wanted to let him know that he probably should not run our interview because of the negative light surrounding my name. We wanted to make sure he didn't endorse a hypocrite, an instrument of unrighteousness. However, I believe he still aired the interview. Maybe he wanted me to understand that a Christian isn't perfect, just forgiven. Maybe he had other reasons. I don't know exactly why, but one thing is certain—being HIS INSTRUMENT has nothing to do with doing interviews and everything to do with your inner views!

During that particular time in my life, I clearly violated the law of HIS INSTRUMENT. I now know firsthand that conforming to this world will destroy a person as surely as fire annihilates flesh, and I am reminded of the fires of hell. As a walking and talking Bible, I must keep my heart and mind set on things above—a heavenly degree.

"Set your mind on things above, not on things on the earth" *(Colossians 3:2).*

VISION RESTORED

When your soul's vision is perfect, you will be seen as one who helps repair the impaired. Like an optician who manufactures vision wear, you too can assist others with their vision. What good would it be to go to an eye doctor who cannot see clearly himself? It is deficiency of vision that brings others to desire your sufficiency of living. Remain in God's hands—in the grip of grace—and you will become an optical instrument that inspires spiritual sight: a higher standard of influence.
U MAY B HIS INSTRUMENT!

Be seen by how you see.

PART III

---

the law of HIS ELEMENT

"Catalyst impact isn't compounded by you, it's simplified by you."

appropriating the law:

Biblical influence is motivational. In God's plan to save man, your "I" is the missing element. Did you know that Christ, the atomic glue, desires to partner up with you? "All things were created through Him and for Him. And He is before all things, and in Him all things consist" (Colossians 1:16b-17). *Thus, simplifying your "I" as an element to be used by Him, through Him, and for Him is understanding that you can do nothing apart from Him. Christ is more than the sum of the "table of elements," He is the stability that holds and unfolds each element. Your biblical awareness of your "Adamic value" is giving every part of you to Christ.*
U MAY B HIS ELEMENT!

In Christ, you are set apart. Without Christ, you will fall apart.

~seeing the law is being the law~

LEGIBLE

-application of the law-

"[...] and the elements will melt with fervent heat [...]"
(II Peter 3:10).

When projecting the law of HIS ELEMENT, we are to be a legible representation of the *character, conversation,* and *conduct* of Jesus Christ.

If not, anything done apart from Him will burn away. As Maya Angelou wisely said, "You may not control all the events that happen to you, but you can decide not to be reduced by them." I love that attitude because it is a personal decision that we all must make in life to impact for the good those people with whom we come into contact regardless of the circumstances that brought us together. And that's why catalyst impact isn't compounded by you, it's simplified by you.

Therefore, I am to be HIS ELEMENT by tapping into the "fundamental substances that consist of atoms of only one kind." That is the actual definition of the word "elements" presented in the periodic table of elements. There is much truth in tapping into that definition of an element, but we must apply it to a different type of "atom." That's right! Our "Atom" is called the "last Adam." So to simplify the law of HIS ELEMENT, I must bear the image and character of the last Adam, the heavenly Man, Jesus Christ: *"And so it is written, 'The first man Adam became a living being.' The last Adam became a life-giving spirit. [...] The first man was of the earth, made of dust; the*

> INFLUENCE:
>
> *It is the characteristic of the good spirit to give courage and strength, consolation, tears, inspiration, and peace, making things easy and removing all obstacles so that the soul may make further progress in good works.*
>
> IGNATIUS OF LOYOLA, 1491-1556

second Man is the Lord from heaven. [...] And as we have borne the image of the man of dust, we shall also bear the image of the heavenly Man" (I Corinthians 15: 45, 47, 49).

Like the periodic table of elements, our Lord and Savior displays various elements that we may exemplify as the only Bible somebody may read. As our last "Atom," I believe that it is His oxygen that first and foremost gives us room to breathe—the oxygen of salvation. Along with "deliverance," the Hebrew word for *salvation* means just that: "room to breathe."

Therefore, like the last Adam, Jesus Christ, when we offer the message of salvation to others, we become the legible oxygen providers to those who may be suffocating around us. Simplifying the law of HIS ELEMENT is not forcing the oxygen mask, the message, upon anyone. Rather, it is influencing somebody to heed your example. Like a flight attendant's demonstration on a plane, as you put on your oxygen mask, you invite others to follow suit or at least to consider the life-saving oxygen presented. Simplified impact.

During the fall of 2009, prior to my sentencing trial, I was blessed with the opportunity to speak at various colleges and high schools. With this platform, in less than two months, I spoke at 34 different schools—reaching over 7,000 students with those assemblies, in addition to the untold number of parents, teachers, and staff members. I wore my shame and pain on my face as I wanted the audience members to see themselves in my shoes. Never to scare them, but to deter them from traveling down the destructive path on which I had traveled.

In a presentation titled, "I'm That Guy," I offered the message "decisions determine destiny" for the students to consider in their individual journey through life. The presentation eventually went viral on the Internet. Having the video of my story being "read" all over the world in over 121 different countries is humbling, but one particular response to my speech was enough for me to realize that my presentation was legible. In an e-mail that I received soon after one of the assemblies, this is what one mother wrote:

"Thank you for sharing your story with the students at Charter Tech High School. You saved my son's life." Her son had attended the "I'm That Guy" presentation on a Friday afternoon. "Later that evening," she wrote, "when leaving a party, he smelled alcohol on the driver's breath and he and his friend got out of the car. The same car was subsequently totaled in an accident, and the seats where he and his friend had been sitting were demolished."

I do not take credit for the results because it is the message that saves lives, not me. I was nothing more than a catalyst for the law of HIS ELEMENT to be the impact, offering a different form of oxygen as well as a message from the Bible. Many of the students may not have realized that they were "reading" the Bible during those assemblies, but I did! I knew that I may have been the only Bible that some may read, thus the exhortation found in Haggai 1:5 to "Consider your ways!" was my attempt at conveying salvation to the listeners.

Remember: Most of the time, our example will be demonstrated in our responses to life's trials. Even if the Bible is not tangibly

> INFLUENCE:
> *Your greatest purpose is found in your greatest pain. Whether you are responsible for the affliction in your life or not, it is your response to the affliction that can instigate somebody else's progression. Practical Insight: Never allow outside influences to deter right response.*
> MATTHEW MAHER, 1984-

presented, like oxygen it does not have to be discernible to be inhaled. On that particular day and at that exact moment, I was the very Bible that this student was able to read. I was legible. And all because I did not allow my circumstances to reduce the invaluable message.

SALT

-illustration of the law-

To simplify the law of HIS ELEMENT, be salt. Be *refreshing*, *reviving*, and *repairing*.

Didn't know salt was an element? Well, it is! The chemical formula for salt is NaCl, sodium chloride. We are to be eatable, readable salt. Don't believe me? Let's see what Jesus said about it. *"You are the salt of the earth; but if the salt loses its flavor, how shall it be seasoned? It is then good for nothing but to be thrown out and trampled underfoot by men" (Matthew 5:13).* In other words, you are the influence of the earth; but if your influence loses its impact, how shall it be useful?

In ancient times, salt was a precious and valuable commodity. For instance, as part of their pay, Roman soldiers were given "salt-money"—money to purchase salt. From "salt-money" comes our word "salary" today. The use of salt as payment also gave rise to expressions such as "not worth his salt." Thus, Jesus' followers, who possess salt-like qualities, are precious and valuable. Let us therefore become salt that we may refresh our world, revive others, and repair that which the devil has broken and putrefied. As the salt of the earth, I have the ability to be fresh in my perspective, and I have the capability of preserving my objective—which is to be a legible read!

One of the main uses of salt throughout history has been as a preservative. Salt is effective in protecting food from decay and the corruption of spoilage; likewise, we are to be effective in protecting our family and culture from moral decay and the corruption of sin. This does not require a judgmental or critical outlook. Anyone can talk down others and point out what is wrong, but the person who talks up, builds up, and offers refreshing, reviving, and repairing words is the one who will be salt-like. To be salt-like is to be Christ-like; to be Christ-like is to be salt-like.

Furthermore, being the only Bible somebody may read requires you to be available for service. Essentially, no one will become thirsty if you are not there to make them thirsty. As salt makes one thirsty, are your words or deeds making anyone thirsty for what you have? I hear this quote often: "You can lead a horse to water, but you can't make him drink." Very true, but as a Christian, it is not our goal to make people drink. We are to make them thirsty for the living water of Jesus Christ. Similar to a commercial for a thirst-quenching beverage, others have to see us drinking in the Word—thereby, "advertising" the Word in order for them to want what we have.

> INSPIRATION:
>
> *On the last day [. . .] Jesus stood and cried out, saying, "If anyone thirsts, let him come to Me and drink. He who believes in Me, as the Scripture has said, out of his heart will flow rivers of living water."*
>
> JOHN 7:37-38

Salt also brings flavor to a meal that would otherwise be bland. In biblical times, salt was a luxury because it was not affordable by everyone. Often, the tasty seasoning was enjoyed only by the wealthiest members of society, such as royalty or those of the noble class. Are we bringing an invaluable flavor to the "food" of those with whom we come into contact? Are you making your company feel noble or royal? Is your conversation tasteful? Is your conduct pleasant? How about your character, is it desirable? Being the salt of the earth is living life so that your savor points to your Savior.

Finally, taking on the qualities of salt, you must also be repairing. And when I say "repair," I mean "mend," "fix," "restore," "revive," *heal.* Salt has remarkable cleansing and healing effects. It can remove stains. In ancient times, it was used to treat wounds. To this day, a saline solution is used by medical personnel to remove bacteria and debris and speed healing. The home remedy for a host of ailments ranging from sore throats and pulled teeth to rashes, cuts, and insect bites and stings includes salt water. Gargle with salt water or jump in the ocean—words of advice that, when followed, are solutions known to dull the pain, dry the ooze, and decrease suffering time.

In addition to being fresh and preserving, you can offer sound advice and counsel toward healing. You can point people in the right direction—not to the salt-shaker, but to the Salt Maker! Everyone needs—and seeks—healing, whether internally

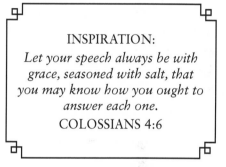

INSPIRATION:
Let your speech always be with grace, seasoned with salt, that you may know how you ought to answer each one.
COLOSSIANS 4:6

or externally. That thirst alone will keep some nonbelievers open to repairing. But unless you live healed, you will have no Christ-appeal. The "appetites of men" are always watching to see what type of additive you are. Hence, to be legible, one must be presentable.

Be legible. Be salt.
Be refreshing. Be reviving. Be repairing.
Be the Bible!

CHARACTER STAMP:

I MAY B salt. Flavorless salt is useless salt. It cannot be seasoned again. You, however, are the salt of the earth, and your flavor is that of your Savior. You season mankind's meals, and you have the element that heals. Let us not forget salt's preservative qualities: You are one who keeps others from the decay of the day. You are more than a "salt shaker"—you are a world-changer.
I MAY B salt.

Bring flavor by your character, healing by your conversation, and preservation by your conduct.

METAL

-illustration of the law-

To simplify the law of HIS ELEMENT, be metal. Be *tested, tried*, and *true*.

The process of refining metal teaches us much about being a tried and true Christian. Faith that is not tested cannot be trusted. Similarly, metal that is not tested cannot be trusted either. A blacksmith subjects his metal piece to the fire in order to purge away the dross from the impure material. Without intense heat, it is impossible to work with metal and make it bend to the will of the blacksmith. When the metal has achieved the change that the blacksmith wants, the metal is then placed in a bucket of cold water to stop the process.

Knowledge of this refining process is crucial in understanding the cross. Christ endured the refining process, and so must I. He, however, endured the cross and the fiery wrath of Hell not because *He* needed to be purified, but so that *I* may be purged of my iniquities—the dross of sin.

> INSPIRATION:
> *For You, O God, have tested us; You have refined us as silver is refined. [. . .] We went through fire and through water; but You brought us out to rich fulfillment.*
> PSALM 66:10, 12

Christ who knew no sin became sin for us (II Corinthians 5:21). If Jesus had to be tested and tried to be found true, how much more can I expect such tribulation to touch my life in order to make me brand-new!

Jesus stated clearly, *"These things I have spoken to you, that in Me you may have peace. In the world you will have tribulation; but be of good cheer, I have overcome the world"* (John 16:33). The original Greek word for "tribulation" means "pressure."

Jesus' promise of peace is the very reason we can *"be of good cheer"* when we are in the furnace of tribulation. Instead of thinking we are being burned up by the heat and destroyed by the pressure, we must know that we are being reformed by the present trial. Such an understanding of the metal-refining process and the cross-aligning process is to know that we are being made into the image of Christ. Though Jesus was God's Son, He learned obedience by the things He suffered (Hebrews 5:1-10). That is what suffering successfully is all about!

> INSPIRATION:
>
> *In this you greatly rejoice, though now for a little while, if need be, you have been grieved by various trials, that the genuineness of your faith, being much more precious than gold that perishes, though it is tested by fire, may be found to praise, honor, and glory at the revelation of Jesus Christ.*
>
> I PETER 1:6-7

I heard it explained this way. A wise blacksmith was asked how he knew his metal had been successfully tested and tried. He replied, "When I begin to see my reflection in the molten state, because this means that all the impurities have been burned away." Likewise, when God begins to see His Son's image and reflection seared into our *character, conduct,* and *conversation,* He knows that the refining process has been successful. However, we cannot forget about the water's cooling after the fire's burning. The refining process is renewed daily by washing in the water of the Word. What good would it do us to be burned with nothing learned?

Understanding the ductile qualities of metal is to understand what it takes to suffer successfully. This comprehension as

HIS ELEMENT is to know that no matter what you are going through, you can be sure that God is working it all together for your good. You WILL be on display as the crucible for nonbelievers, which is why it is crucial to know that **U MAY B THE ONLY BIBLE SOMEBODY READS!** Are you remaining legible by the way you're handling your crucible?

Without the refining process, the metal remains hardened in its original form. The pollutants that degrade the metal will remain embedded unless removed by the formidable methods. So in order to be usable, one must be fusible. One must be willing to go through the fiery trials, heated times, and burning days in order to be purged of all dross. Being the only Bible that somebody may read is knowing the hard times are not counted as loss. Will you be metal and do more for Christ, which means never settle for less than God's best for your life!

> INSPIRATION:
> *He will sit as a refiner and purifier of silver; He will purify the sons of Levi, and purge them as gold and silver, that they may offer to the Lord an offering in righteousness.*
> MALACHI 3:3

Be legible. Be metal.
Be tested. Be tried. Be true.
Be the Bible!

CHARACTER STAMP:

*I MAY B metal. Metal, when refined and purified, is essentially
justified and glorified. The metal must be tested in order to
be trusted. Likewise, your "I" must be tested to be trusted
so you can see your worth and value. The Refiner must place
the metal in the crucible, not to ruin—but to make sure it is
fusible and usable. God, however, already knows the lustrous
quality within you, but He will pass you through the fire to
show YOU this hue.*
I MAY B *metal.*

*Realize God trusted you with trouble, not to make you or
break you—but to reveal you.*

STONE

-illustration of the law-

To simplify the law of HIS ELEMENT, be a stone. Be *separate*, *sculpted*, and *solid*.

Whether we consider a limestone statue, a granite countertop, a marble pillar or a diamond gemstone, such stones did not begin in their current form. They were taken from the earth as a bulk of mineral matter. In order to become a product with purpose, the stone had to be separated from its environment. We, too, must be removed in order to be usable and readable in our environments.

A Christian must separate him- or herself from the world. Speaking in prayer to God the Father, Jesus said, "[My disciples] are not of the world, just as I am not of the world. Sanctify them (Set them apart and declare them holy) by Your truth. Your Word is truth" (John 17:16-17, parenthetical emphasis added).

> INSPIRATION:
> *He who overcomes, I will make him a pillar in the temple of God [. . .].*
> REVELATION 3:12a

Set apart and not set in the hard ways of the world. Not set in stone. No! Being the only Bible that somebody may read is being the one who is sanctified by integrity and righteousness. Separated from the world in order to be regulated by the Word. Standing out from the crowd for godly reasons, and standing up in spite of the crowd for Christ-like reasons.

What's "a reason" from the Word? It's motivation based on your conviction and faith. It's your disposition of grace. It's being so soft and gentle that you're rock-solid. It's being meek, which is far from being weak. A Word reason loves God, and loves others as you love yourself. And that's the reason you can say, "Word up!"

The Word tells us that we are "living stones," a chip off of Christ's block, being built up as God's building project. Therefore, whether we are dealing with sandpaper people or chisel challenges, we are to use every circumstance as an opportunity to be sculpted into the image of Christ. As a stone, your personality can never shine like a diamond until you are willing to be cut—allowing God to fashion you through what you're going through. If left in the hardened state, a stony heart will make you nothing more than a hard read.

> INSPIRATION:
> *Coming to Him as to a living stone, rejected indeed by men, but chosen by God and precious, you also, as living stones, are being built up a spiritual house, a holy priesthood, to offer up spiritual sacrifices to God through Jesus Christ.*
> I PETER 2:4-5

Furthermore, nothing piques the curiosity of a nonbeliever more than your ability to build blocks instead of throwing rocks. It's easy to gossip about others—tearing them down and criticizing their faults. But being like stone is about being solid in content and concrete in words and actions. Seek to build up and support others—establish and edify them with encouragement.

Do people hear you cursing in tone; or are your words smooth as marble stone? Are you the one condemning and stoning; or are you like Jesus, drawing a line in the shifting sand and using truth to take a solid stand?

You never know who is looking or who is listening in the rock quarry of life. That is why being a stone is about being separated from the world, sculpted by the Word, and solid in your work.

You will affect your nonbelieving friends and neighbors by the way you see them and treat them. Like God the Creator, and like an artistic stone-cutter, see others as the

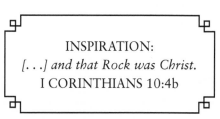

INSPIRATION:
[. . .] and that Rock was Christ.
I CORINTHIANS 10:4b

finished product already made complete and perfect in Christ. Treat them with precise and loving taps that chip away at their resistance to the gospel. Be the stone pillar that they can lean on through hard times. Be the only Bible they may read by being a gem to them—caring with clarity, and valuable by adding value to them.

Be legible. Be a stone.
Be separated. Be sculpted. Be solid.
Be the Bible

CHARACTER STAMP:

I MAY B a stone. We mine stone from a quarry, detaching it
from the earth's hold of it, to be used in the earth with a new
mold or fit. Diamond. Marble. Granite. You are the product
of how you spend your time after your birthstone and before
your gravestone. Polished to be felt. Cut to be brilliant.
Formed to fit. You are detached from the earth to be used in
the earth—but made fit for heaven.
I MAY B a stone.

Learn to look beyond the gravestone.

HELIUM

-illustration of the law-

To simplify the law of HIS ELEMENT, be like helium. Be *uplifting* and *laughing*.

I bet you never thought that being like helium would be an admirable Christian characteristic! Well, it is, even though I don't quite recall the last time someone referred to me as being like helium. But the more I think about the effects of this gaseous chemical element, the more I hope to be helium-like.

Helium is the second-lightest element. In other words, not heavy. That's right! Did you know that helium is lighter than air? Which means: If we are to be like helium, we should not be weighed down—made "heavy"—by our burdens nor should we feel bound to the earth (too comfortable in this world or too complacent with our placement on this planet). However, we ought not to be airheads when it comes to our mission on earth.

So, we must keep our eyes lifted up as helium lifts up a balloon, heaven-bound, that we may not get caught up in the things of this world. Being the only Bible that somebody may read is living life in light of eternity, knowing that this eternal hope is what keeps us afloat. The hope of heaven is a promise that should keep you pressing forward by faith no matter what you are facing. I've heard it said that it gets greater later. And when you keep your perspective high and lifted up on Christ the Risen Savior, there will be no temporary circumstance that can deflate you.

Don't get me wrong: Being like helium has nothing to do with the pride that puffs up, and everything to do with the hot-air-balloon ride that lifts up. Do you lift up people with encouragement and instruction? Is your presence lifting or sifting? Are you one who elevates the surrounding conditions by bringing others to a new level of thinking; or are you one who elevates himself by looking down at those around, leaving others behind and below?

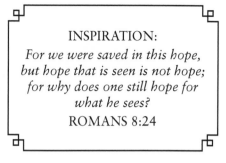

INSPIRATION:

For we were saved in this hope, but hope that is seen is not hope; for why does one still hope for what he sees?

ROMANS 8:24

As Christians, we should be the most approachable people in the world. People should not be turned off by our presence nor turned away by our countenance. Our face should be read as joyous and inspirational; and by our helium-like laugh, we ought to be contagious. We know that Jesus was this way because he criticized the religious leaders for their lack of love, justice, mercy, and faithfulness to God—in spite of their robotic obedience to the letter of the law. Furthermore, God the Father anointed His Son with the oil of gladness (Hebrews 1:9).

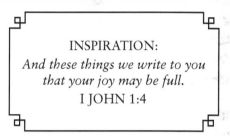

INSPIRATION:

And these things we write to you that your joy may be full.

I JOHN 1:4

Jesus could lift up those around Him by the light of His eyes alone—a mere look was enough to inspire devotion and change in Zaccheus, for example (Luke 19:1-10). As Jesus was being read by the lost, the sick, and the suffering, they found His demeanor—His air, His attitude, and His appearance—legible enough to go to Him.

What happens when you inhale helium and then begin to talk? Your pitch rises, and laughter follows. Such should be the case whenever you are around. Your advice, counsel, and

> **INSPIRATION:**
>
> *Then our mouth was filled with laughter, and our tongue with singing. Then they said among the nations, "The Lord has done great things for them." The Lord has done great things for us, and we are glad.*
>
> PSALM 126

instruction should be inspirational. The Greek word for "inspiration" means "God-breathed." Thus, when our countenance and conversation are God-breathed, the content will have a helium effect. *Uplifting. Inspirational. Motivational. Relational. And profitable for contemplation and instruction. Most importantly, legible!*

Be legible. Be helium.
Be uplifting. Be laughing!
Be the Bible!

CHARACTER STAMP:

I MAY B helium. Helium is not affected by the earth's pull. Its law of occurrence is greater than the law of gravity. It lifts up and is light; it is the gaseous chemical that takes flight. Thus, like helium, it is your countenance that must always lift up others. The peace within you should make heavy matters light. Make intentional effort to keep your mind stayed on God, for He gives you His perfect peace in return.
I MAY B helium.

Rise above the pull with the peace that pushes up.

ILLEGIBLE

-violation of the law-

"But now after you have known God, or rather are known by God, how is it that you turn again to the weak and beggarly elements, to which you desire again to be in bondage?"
(Galatians 4:9).

I may have begun with a time when I was legible as HIS EL-EMENT, but there were plenty of times when I was illegible. It wasn't that I was just unreadable; in fact, I was combustible. Clearly agitated. Thus, it is fitting that I share such examples with you that you may learn from my destructive use of the element oxygen and do better.

You can never hear enough negative examples because they can persuasively keep you from paying the pricey tuition that comes with certain educational experiences. An understanding of the periodic table of elements should be enough to keep you from conducting dangerous experiments, such as the one I am about to share.

Contrary to the positive use of oxygen in LEGIBLE, which was as an element of salvation, there was a time when I used it as an element of combustion. In the movie *Backdraft*, starring Kurt Russell, the plot revolves around the explosive combustion that occurs during a fire when oxygen is

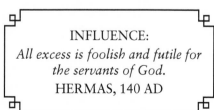

INFLUENCE:
All excess is foolish and futile for the servants of God.
HERMAS, 140 AD

rapidly reintroduced into an oxygen-depleted environment by the sudden opening of a door or window. The same concept applies to this situation. You see, I knew there was a fire raging on the other side of this "door," yet I decided to open it. My arrival was the element that caused the flames of tension to detonate like a backdraft—burning everyone in the vicinity.

It was the fall of 2007. I had just completed my first season as a professional soccer player in Raleigh, N.C. I then underwent hernia surgery before traveling back home to southern New Jersey, where I was instructed by the doctors to simply rest and recuperate prior to the resumption of soccer. In other words, the injury alone should have been enough to keep me from doing anything extensive in motion—but it wasn't enough.

My next soccer season was to be played for the N.J. Ironmen in the Major Indoor Soccer League (MISL). In the meantime, I decided to spend a weekend in Philadelphia—the city of my alma mater, Temple University, and the location for the birthday celebration of a good friend. I had not seen my old friends in a while, so it seemed like a nice opportunity for a group of us to meet, eat, and catch up before going out together for the night.

The evening progressed with a fine air of fellowship, until the wind blew in another element—the "X" factor, an ex-girlfriend from my college years. It was nice to see her, and we chatted briefly—catching up on each other's life. Then entered her old friends from home.

It was clear that they had a problem with me, and soon my friends and her friends—two groups of guys who refused to back down from a confrontation—were in an altercation. A fire had been ignited.

As I jumped into a taxi, planning to leave the flammable situation, in jumped my ex. I requested that the driver proceed to her apartment. After dropping her off and making sure she was safely home, I asked the taxi driver to take me to where I and my friends were staying for the night.

When I arrived, my friends were there, and we talked about what happened. Fortunately, nobody was hurt so the fire burns had apparently been avoided. Then the phone rang. The caller was my ex's new boyfriend. He had not even been present at the scene of the "fire," but these flames were just getting started.

I should have stayed where I was, at least allowed my hernia injury to keep me still. I should have allowed the distance to give me "room to breathe." I should have remembered that I might be the only Bible this guy—and others involved in the situation—would ever read. I should have, but I didn't. I have no excuses for my actions in this dispute, but I can tell you with hindsight 20/20 that my ego kept me from being able to ignore the antagonizing. My pride caused me to respond to a previously sparked fire that was now oxygen-depleted and should have been left to dwindle with the only element that was missing: the oxygen of my presence. I reacted to the challenge by accepting his invitation to meet.

> INFLUENCE:
> *When we try to make a decision, we have one soul which is torn between conflicting wills. Some say that there are two opposing minds within us, one good and the other bad, and that they are in conflict because they spring from two opposing substances and principles.*
> ST. AUGUSTINE, 354-430 AD

I may have been taunted into showing up at "the fire," but I didn't have to go. I knew what was on the other side of "the door." I knew the doorknob was hot, and I smelled smoke. Yet, I opened the door and set off the backdraft. I introduced the element—myself—that caused the altercation to progress into devastation.

I showed up in spite of my better judgment. Oxygen rushed in, and with a hard blow I broke his jaw that night. I can tell you one thing for certain: the law of HIS ELEMENT has nothing to do with reckless combustion, and everything to do with controlled composition. Simplifying the law of HIS ELEMENT is being one who takes oxygen away from a destructive fire, which suffocates the flames. Simplifying the law of HIS ELEMENT is being one who uses oxygen to provide "room to breathe." Remember, catalyst impact isn't compounded by you, it's simplified by you.

INFLUENCE:
There is a civil war going on inside of every person. Spirit vs. flesh. The more we wage our own attacks, the more the flesh fights us back. Victory isn't found in the strategy of our mission. No! Victory is succeeded by the humility of our submission. Practical Insight: What side will win the more? The side you feed more. Feed the spirit.
MATTHEW MAHER, 1984-

On that particular night and at that exact moment, I violated the law of HIS ELEMENT. I now know firsthand that the more oxygen added to an already volatile situation, the hotter the flames, the more intense the fire. Our world is the only known planet where fire can burn because it is the only planet that has sufficient oxygen. Spiritually, that is why I must not be of this world.

"Do not love the world or the things in the world. If anyone loves the world, the love of the Father is not in him" (I John 2:15).

VISION RESTORED

Not all elements can be seen, but that does not mean they don't exist. Therefore, you may not see the elements of the Spirit you cultivate, but you will be the manifestation of elements as they elevate. Manifestation often comes without observation, such as breathing oxygen. You cannot see the oxygen, but that doesn't mean you are not breathing the gas. Thus, your vision should not be dependent upon what you see in the world, but more so by what you foresee in the Word. Align your "I"-sight to see what God sees.
U MAY B HIS ELEMENT!

Let your faith see what your eyes cannot.

PART IV

---

the law of HIS LIGHT

"Wielding heaven's influence has intensity behind it—the arrival of light:
As above, so below."

appropriating the law:

Biblical influence is radical. Jesus said, "You are the light of the world." *Radiating the law of HIS LIGHT, then, is understanding that you must illuminate your surroundings—the world—and, further, that the darkness of hell must be present for heaven's influence through you to be seen most clearly. Darkness, therefore, is needed to detect this law. And if you're seriously committed to let your light shine before men on earth, then they will see your good works and glorify your Father in heaven. As above, so below.*
U MAY B HIS LIGHT!

Recognize that darkness is the prerequisite to light.

~seeing the law is being the law~

LEGIBLE

-application of the law-

"You are the light of the world [...]" (Matthew 5:14).

When projecting the law of HIS LIGHT, we are to be a legible representation of the *character, conversation,* and *conduct* of Jesus Christ.

I like to say that light is of no use unless there is darkness. Light is needed to illuminate. Light is necessary for true sight. Therefore, it is usually in the darkness of life that we learn best the effectiveness of light. I am to reflect the law of HIS LIGHT by simply letting HIS LIGHT shine through me. It is so simple, it is profound. Jesus said, *"Let your light so shine before men, that they may see your good works and glorify your Father in heaven" (Matthew 5:16).*

In Matthew 5, Jesus instructs us to "let"; to "let" is to do nothing but allow. Thus, we are to simply and profoundly allow HIS LIGHT to shine out of us. Nothing more; nothing less. When we reflect the law of HIS LIGHT, we illuminate Christ. We reveal the Word. We become the transparent Bible that somebody may read by "letting" God radiate His glory through our lives; by "letting" heavens influence change lives. That's the law of HIS LIGHT.

Wait! Surely, to be legible as HIS LIGHT we must be good-looking and extremely talented, right? Wrong! Like Jesus said, we are to simply, yet successfully, "let." *"Let your light so shine before men"* is not a hard commandment, but an easy empowerment. It's HIS LIGHT. We just have to "let" it shine into our world, that our good works will bring God glory. That's that! Being HIS LIGHT is not a competition or a struggle. It is allowing somebody to read the Bible by our light, especially in times of darkness.

INFLUENCE:

The Inner Light, the Inward Christ, is no mere doctrine, belonging peculiarly to a small religious fellowship, to be accepted or rejected as a mere belief. It is the living Center of Reference for all Christian souls and Christian groups [. . .] A practicing Christian must above all be one who practices the perpetual return of the soul into the inner sanctuary, who brings the world into its Light and rejudges it, who brings the Light into the world with all its turmoil and its fitfulness and re-creates it. To the reverent exploration of this practice we now address ourselves.

THOMAS KELLY, 1893-1941

As I pen this book in the darkness of prison, I have found the "let" instruction both promising and empowering. Had I not "let" HIS LIGHT shine, I would have "let" myself whine. In prison, darkness is the default setting that usually goes unchecked. But I knew something biblical before I even arrived in prison: that darkness is nothing more than the absence of light. The absence of moral integrity. So from the beginning of my prison term, I knew I had to take a Genesis approach: *Then God said, "Let there be light"; and there was light. And God saw the light, that it was good; and God divided the light from the darkness (Genesis 1: 3-4).*

Most every morning for over three years, I have made it a habit to begin my day at the front table on my prison tier. Usually I am sitting there, with my Bible and devotional books, before the automatic lights shoot on at 6 A.M. The sudden luminescence acts as an alarm clock, rousing many from their slumber, but the majority responds contrary to the light's purpose. Instead of embracing it, they fight the light. They resist it. They shut it out. They prefer the darkness.

It is during this period of awakening that prison's darkness is most visible. Shuffling like the walking dead, inmates head to the bathroom to wash up their outward presentation, but not to waken their inward illumination. More fights break out in the early morning due to bad moods and crude attitudes. It was because of the Genesis approach that I found two words to be the only Bible many of my peers would ever read.

While they are still rubbing the sleep out of their eyes, I make it a point to tell each person, "Good morning!" This cheerful greeting is a foreign language in this alien land, but I learned very quickly that there was no other opportunity to set the tone of the day than at the day's beginning. Saying "good morning" may not sound like a big deal from where you read this book, but it was a potentially dangerous ordeal for me. You see, prisoners do not believe there is anything good about a morning in prison, and telling them differently could be viewed as an aggressive taunt. They may then violently attempt to show you otherwise.

Nonetheless, and in spite of the darkness and possible negative consequences, I have delivered this positive wish for a good morning each day in order to be a legible read to my peers. If I were already sitting at the table with my Bible open, then why wouldn't I open up the Bible's pages to my fellow inmates with a kindly "good morning"? I do not have to force it out. I do not have to quote extensive verses. I do not even have to engage in difficult conversations. None of that is necessary to just "let." I only have to let HIS LIGHT shine through me by turning the switch on inside me. Simply "let" God, and leave the consequences to Him.

It is easy, actually, and just as God did in the beginning, I too was able to divide light from darkness. As a result, *"God saw the light, that it was good,"* and it wasn't long at all before my environment began to lighten up as well—literally and emotionally. The atmosphere was flipped because of two simple words at the break of day: "Good morning!"

> INFLUENCE:
>
> *Christianity means community through Jesus Christ and in Jesus Christ. No Christian community is more or less than this . Whether it be a brief, single encounter or the daily fellowship of years, Christian community is only this. We belong to one another only through and in Jesus Christ.*
> DIETRICH BONHOEFFER, 1906-1945

I remember doing time early on in my bid with an older gentleman named Johnny. I was unaware that my daily greetings were affecting him until he was moved to another housing unit in the prison. In the mess hall one morning, he sought me out. He sat down beside me and said, "No one says 'good morning' to me on my new tier. Your words set my day up, Matthew. And I just wanted to let you know to never stop smiling. Keep being a light."

I did not fully grasp the importance of what Johnny was telling me until these same words were echoed by other inmates at various times throughout this journey. Truthfully, it was because of those two words combined with a smile that the law of HIS LIGHT was revealed in a dark setting. As above, so below. Thus, I was able to conquer the setting by simply "letting."

> INFLUENCE:
>
> *Your presence has the power to make others feel significant. Never diminish this influence. Remember, whether directly or indirectly, our conviction is always speaking. Practical Insight: Be intentional in your countenance. You never know how a bright look or light greeting can illuminate your surroundings.*
> MATTHEW MAHER, 1984-

Each day in this place, beginning with the morning, I try to be the Bible that my peers will read. I legibly say, "Good morning." Though some may never pick up the Bible, you never know who is picking up the Bible in you. On a dark night, the human eye can see a candle flame flickering up to 30 miles away. You may be unaware of how far your flickering flame—a simple, consistent, cheerful, and positive greeting—can go to being a clear read of HIS LIGHT.

CANDLE

-illustration of the law-

To radiate the law of HIS LIGHT, be a candle. Be *mobile*, *melting*, and *meek*.

Be a candle. Even a birthday candle the size of a matchstick gives great delight; and in a power outage, a person is glad and grateful to find an insignificant stub. Why? Because it is not the candle's size, color or scent that matters and makes it serviceable. It is the flame that burns from the wick. Thus, the purpose of the candle is visible only when it is lit.

We often think that for God to adequately use us, we must be lighthouses—monumentally significant and prominently displayed. We need to see the importance of the modest. That miniature birthday candle turns a pastry into a party. The stub gives direction as well as illumination. A single candle turns the routine into romantic.

One of the main reasons we buy and use candles is because of the fact that they are mobile. They are easily accessible and transportable, kept in drawers and closets for a quick grab. You can take a candle to any location without worrying about the need for an electrical outlet, gasoline or a battery. Candles are usable and movable. Therefore, to be

INSPIRATION:
But His word was in my heart like a burning fire shut up in my bones;I was weary of holding it back, and I could not.
JEREMIAH 20:9b

like candles, we should be accessible, mobile, and usable in any environment. And like the candle's flame, we have God's Word in our hearts to warm and enlighten in any setting. Our glowing countenance ought to make those around us comfortable.

The natural result of a burning wick is a melted candle. Eventually, a candle consumes itself. This is the desired outcome for one who allows God's fire to burn within. There is a great quote, whose author is unknown, about good teachers that should be equally true and applicable to Christ's followers: "A good [Christian] is like a candle—it consumes itself to light the way for others."

> INSPIRATION:
> For whosoever desires to save his life will lose it, but whoever loses his life for My sake will find it. For what profit is it to a man if he gains the whole world, and loses his own soul? Or what will a man give in exchange for his soul?
> MATTHEW 16: 25-26

But be careful! "Wick watchers" will try to snuff you out. Shut you up or shut you down! But the more you die to your fleshly self, like a candle consuming itself, the more effectively and efficiently you will live in the Spirit. A Spirit-filled follower is one who is selfless, rather than one who is self-absorbed.

A candle cannot light itself; but when its wick is touched by the flame, it serves its purpose meekly. Hence, to be like a candle is to be lit by the Word and to move in such a humble manner that the focus is on HIS LIGHT—not on your color, shape or design. Some candles have pleasant aromas within them; so do we! However, in order to release such sweet scents, our wick must be set ablaze for the fragrance of *Christ* to burn forth as *self* melts away.

> INSPIRATION:
> For our God is a consuming fire.
> HEBREWS 12:29

Being the only Bible that somebody may read is

knowing what it takes to be a good read. It's knowing that we live in a world cloaked in darkness, powered artificially by lights that fail. Battery-power *status* that is eventually depleted. Gasoline-fueled *money* that eventually runs out. Electrical *respect* that is eventually cut. However, when you possess HIS LIGHT and the glow doesn't go, the world will desire your source. Be ready to faithfully explain.

Be legible. Be a candle.
Be mobile. Be melting. Be meek.
Be the Bible!

CHARACTER STAMP:

I MAY B a candle. A candle burns to produce light, but without the fire the candle is just wax and wick. Thus, the only way for the candle to be consumed while illuminating is to allow the burning flame to have its glorious way. Likewise, when you truly desire to die to self and be set aglow, you must allow the burning fire to "melt" self for Christ to show.
I MAY B a candle.

Let self melt down for Christ's fire to rise up.

GLOW STICK

-illustration of the law-

To radiate the law of HIS LIGHT, be a glow stick. Be *bought*, *broken*, and *blameless*.

I'm sure that at some point in your life you possessed or handled a glow stick. Whether for good fun or emergency purposes, every type of glow stick has to be broken before it can give light. The brokenness occurs on the inside. Within the plastic tube are chemicals housed in separate containers. When the plastic tube is bent or flexed, the inner containers break and release chemicals that—when combined—emit the "glow."

Understanding brokenness and its importance in radiating HIS LIGHT results in the very humility and dependence that brings the Bible to life. It is in God's hands that He blesses us, breaks us, and gives us back as a blessing to others. Without the breaking, the shining of the blessing through the giving could never be seen. No matter how roughly life has handled you, when you know Whose hands ultimately hold you, you can be certain that the breaking was intended to release your light.

Being the only Bible that somebody may read is knowing that you were bought at a price; and because our body and spirit are not our own—but God's—we ought to live

> INSPIRATION:
> *For You do not desire sacrifice, or else I would give it; You do not delight in burnt offering. The sacrifices of God are a broken spirit, a broken and contrite heart—these, O God, You will not despise.*
> PSALM 51: 16-17

like we have been purchased. We have been bought to be put to good use.

> **INSPIRATION:**
> *For you were bought at a price; therefore glorify God in your body and in your spirit, which are God's.*
> I CORINTHIANS 6:20

You don't buy a glow stick unless you have a purpose for this unique light—which is portable, waterproof, inexpensive, disposable, and generated without bulb or battery. You may want it for fun—as a party decoration, to wave at a music concert or to signal others while swimming underwater. You may want it for safety or in case of emergency—to light a dark pathway while walking or alert others to danger or the scene of an accident. Regardless of the reason, you were the one who bought the glow stick, and therefore you had the right to break it and use it for the purpose of your choice. Likewise, because God has purchased us with His Son's blood, He has a right to break us and put our unique light to use according to His own purpose.

At this point, you may be wondering, "How is a glow stick *blameless*?" And I'd have to explain the biblical meaning of blameless. To be blameless is to be filled with integrity—straightforward and ethically straight. Being blameless is not being sinless, but a believer's life is free from habitual sinful behaviors because he or she is motivated and controlled by Christ's moral principles and filled with the right substance: righteousness.

Consider the substance inside a glow stick. The integrity of the mixture must be *blameless* in order for the *brokenness* to produce a brightness. The chemical blend must be precise to bring the glow to life—and that's exactly what will be noticed in your life. Remaining filled with integrity regardless of the circumstances in which you find yourself—wherever and with whomever you may be.

Without having the right contents on the inside, nobody will enjoy your presence on the outside. Your influence on those around you will be most legible when you know the power and glory is inside of you. Tap into it by allowing God to snap you into it. Even Jesus was broken!

> INSPIRATION:
> *Do all things without complaining and disputing, that you may become blameless and harmless, children of God without fault in the midst of a crooked and perverse generation, among whom you shine as lights in the world.*
> PHILIPPIANS 2: 14-15

Be legible. Be a glow stick.
Be bought. Be broken. Be blameless.
Be the Bible!

CHARACTER STAMP:

I MAY B a glow stick. A glow stick must be broken to be brightened. Its luminescent presence can be seen not in its original state, but only in its agitated state. The fluids on the inside of the glow stick must be stimulated to be illuminated. Thus, you must remind yourself to "stir up the gift of God which is in you" (II Timothy 1:6) in order to have this gift radiate out of you.
I MAY B a glow stick.

Make the effort to exercise your gift within to execute excellence without.

MOON

-illustration of the law-

To radiate the law of HIS LIGHT, be the moon. Be *reflective* and *real*.

The sun of the nighttime sky is the stuff of romance and poetry. Bob Dylan wrote: "The pale moon rose in all its glory." Dean Martin crooned: "When the moon hits your eye like a big pizza pie, that's amore!"

The moon may look like a painting against a black backdrop or a one-dimensional photograph, but it's real. You can question the first moon landing and debate whether that event was a hoax, as many conspiracy theorists do. But no one questions the actual existence of the earth's natural satellite because no one can deny the sight of reflective light.

That is why it is the moon that I must strive to be—because then I know that my light has nothing to do with me. The moon is not producing the light that we see at night. Though surrounded by darkness, the moon's silver illumination is a mirror-like, reflective response of the sun's glory. Without the sun, the moon would remain in darkness.

INSPIRATION:
But we all, with unveiled face, beholding as in a mirror the glory of the Lord, are being transformed into the same image from glory to glory, just as by the Spirit of the Lord.
II CORINTHIANS 3:18

Likewise, we remain in darkness when we are without the Son's glory. Without

HIS LIGHT, we cannot shine; and we only show a light-deprived and depraved side—our dark side. We need the Son's light in our lives that we may reflect HIS LIGHT in the darkness of the world. Is anyone enjoying your moon-light? Are nonbelievers looking into the black backdrop of your life and seeing your bright side or your dark side?

The only way the moon can be blocked from the sun's powerful light is when the earth gets in the way. When the world gets between the sun and the moon, it's called a lunar eclipse. The earth's shadow then obscures the moon. If you, like the moon, live your life as a mirror of God's Son, then your reflection will highlight the paths of those walking in the dark. The moon cannot take credit for its light; likewise, when you help those living in the darkness, you must make it clear that you are nothing without HIS LIGHT.

Astronomers and astrologers read the sky for signs and answers. Thus, being the moon as the only Bible that somebody may read is leading them to a telescopic conclusion: a sight that brings something invisible into view. Your example ought to close the distance between those

> INSPIRATION:
> *For it is God who commanded light to shine out of darkness, who has shone in our hearts to give the light of the knowledge of the glory of God in the face of Jesus Christ.*
> II CORINTHIANS 4:6

who are gazing at your "sky" (your life) through "the lens of your telescope" (your conduct) and the God of the Bible's compassionate character and loving nature.

Many are scared of God and afraid to read the Bible because they don't understand Him or His word. Therefore, it is crucial for us to bring misunderstanding and misinterpretation to light. One of the biggest turn-offs for nonbelievers is hypocrisy. Fakin' da funk. When you know your humble position in the solar system of life, you don't have to exhaust yourself being a planet you're not. You don't have to force yourself into the mold of another orbit. No! You just have to be real—you can't fake real.

> **INSPIRATION:**
> *This is the message which we have heard from Him and declare to you, that God is light and in Him is no darkness at all. If we say that we have fellowship with Him, and walk in darkness, we lie and do not practice the truth. But if we walk in the light as He is in the light, we have fellowship with one another, and the blood of Jesus Christ His Son cleanses us from all sin.*
> I JOHN 1:5-7

Being the moon is giving the sun all the glory; be the moon, and give the Son all the glory, honor, and praise in all that you do. Being moon-like isn't about causing people to be moonstruck nor is it about causing them to "howl" like "we're wolves" (werewolves!). It is simply reflecting Christ's light. Christ is the center of a believer's life as the sun is the center of our solar system; let us reflect HIS LIGHT to a dark night. Now that's a legible sight!

Be legible. Be the moon.
Be reflective. Be real.
Be the Bible!

CHARACTER STAMP:

I MAY B the moon. Without the sun's brilliant light, we would not be able to see the moon at night. Its glow in the blackness of night is strictly because of its reflective properties. It remains dark without the sun in sight, and so do we without the Son's light. Therefore, your "I" must remain aligned with the Son in order to be a reflection of the Son.
I MAY B the moon.

Be grateful of your position in the Son for it grants you permission with the Father.

STARS

-illustration of the law-

To radiate the law of HIS LIGHT, be a star. Be *special*, *steady*, and *shining*.

There is a saying: "Shoot for the moon. Even if you miss, you will land among the stars." Why not just be a star? Just be who you are, who God created you to be: special, with no other being out there like you.

God created you to perform a certain task, to shine a certain light, to be a special delight. You may not be as visible as other people, but you are still a star in God's eyes. And you better know that people are looking at you. That's right! "Star gazers" will turn their attention to you during the nightfall—when you are in the midst of a dark time. A tragedy, a hardship or affliction. So here is the ultimate question: Are you legible?

Are you viewed as steady and shining during the night of adversity? When you know your stardom finds its intensity in God's Word, then you will face the darkness successfully. You will sparkle like a diamond on black velvet. The black background enhances

> INSPIRATION:
> *But recall the former days in which, after you were illuminated, you endured a great struggle with sufferings: partly while you were made a spectacle both by reproaches and tribulations [...] Therefore do not cast away your confidence, which has great reward. For you have need of endurance, so that after you have done the will of God, you may receive the promise.*
> HEBREWS 10:32-33a, 35-36

> **INSPIRATION:**
> *Arise, shine; for your light has come! And the glory of the Lord is risen upon you.*
> ISAIAH 60:1

the radiance. Like a star in the night sky, you, too, will appear bright: shining, not whining; glimmering, not whimpering; heavenly handled, not heavily dismantled.

Did you know that stars are always in motion? Some move at tremendous speeds, but they are so far away that their position appears to be fixed. Steady. There is much to learn from this reliable disposition—because even though much motion is happening all around you, and much commotion is happening inside you, as a star you are always seen as steady and fixed. No matter how dark the night may be, no matter how rapid your trajectory, you are stable in mind. Unwavering and trustworthy.

> **INSPIRATION:**
> *Those who are wise shall shine like the brightness of the firmament, and those who turn many to righteousness like the stars forever and ever.*
> DANIEL 12:3

Don't let your neighbors read the wrong stars and false prophesies. Be the star that they read—shining forth in faith, a constellation of hope.

Be legible. Be a star.
Be special. Be steady. Be shining.
Be the Bible!

CHARACTER STAMP:

I MAY B a star. A star is a celestial body that appears as a fixed point of light. If lost, one can use a star for guidance to find one's way. Consider the biblical wise men who were brought to the Messiah based on prophetic direction. It was a star that led them where God needed them. Thus, like a star, it is your fixed position in the Word that gives biblical direction to the world.
I MAY B a star.

Be the fixed point of light to assist somebody through a dark night.

ILLEGIBLE

-violation of the law-

"The night is far spent, the day is at hand. Therefore let us cast off the works of darkness, and let us put on the armor of light" (Romans 13:12).

I may have begun with a time when I was legible as HIS LIGHT, but there were also plenty of times when I was illegible. It wasn't that I was just unreadable; in fact, I was unpredictable. Clearly fed up! Thus, it is fitting that I share such examples with you that you may learn from my snuffing of HIS LIGHT and learn to be "letting" HIS LIGHT shine.

In the following situation, instead of allowing HIS LIGHT to shine through me, I snuffed it out. I "let" the night inside of me have its dark way. Only for a moment and only by the stifling of two words, yet it was enough to black-out the law of HIS LIGHT. Unlike my LEGIBLE example of "good morning," these two words of mine were an ILLEGIBLE example, and they were enough to cancel out a million kind and encouraging words thereafter. "SHUT UP!"

"Shut up!" I blurted out sharply and aggressively. I was exhausted, but I'll get back to that in a minute. You must first understand that though this testimony begins with those two words, it was with those two words that my

> INFLUENCE:
> *Mitigate violent attacks by gentle applications.*
> IGNATIUS, died circa 117AD

legibility and influence ended. From that moment on, I knew that I had written out the wrong example to my peers. No matter how much Bible I lived out after this experience, those two words automatically cancelled me out. I tried to clean up what I messed up, but it was too late because of the two words I abruptly blurted out: "Shut up!"

I was exhausted from several straight hours of reading and studying, which transitioned into a couple more hours of writing and contemplating. After my morning duties, I only had a moment to gather myself together in prayer before leading the Bible study on the tier prior to lunch. Then I was right back into writing and more exhaustive thinking well into the afternoon. The only time I stopped was to readjust my posture in the chair. I worked nonstop for over 12 hours—until my fellow inmates left the tier for dinner in the mess hall.

When they left, I ate and then decided to close "my office" and unwind by returning to my bed and resting my mind. Just as I was getting comfortable on my 2-inch prison mattress, everyone came storming back onto the tier. And in came my bunkmates. Needless to say, there is no private space, and conversations can take place directly across your bed and over your head while you lay there.

I felt myself allowing frustration to kick in. I usually disregarded the pointless chatter or disturbing noise on the tier at all hours of the day and night, but this time ... This "Temperpedic" moment did not prevent me from losing my temper. I held back a while, but with each passing

> **INFLUENCE:**
>
> *If we are not our own, but the Lord's, it is clear to what purpose all our deeds must be directed. We are not our own, therefore neither our reason nor our will should guide us in our thoughts and actions. We are not our own, therefore we should not seek what is only expedient to the flesh. We are not our own, therefore let us forget ourselves and our own interests as far as possible.*
>
> JOHN CALVIN, 1509-1564

moment and with each senseless comment shouted above the blasting music of a nearby radio, I turned my "let" into fret. I allowed my exasperation to slowly but surely dim HIS LIGHT.

All I had to do was "let" it out in prayer in order to keep the armor of light illuminated. But I let it get to me. And this "let" led to an extinguishing of HIS LIGHT. And when the light is turned off, darkness reigns and heaven's influence wanes!

"Shut up!" With those two words, shouted condescendingly, I added to the din and contradicted my example before my tier mates. How do I know this? Because one of my bunkies pulled out the trump card that every nonbeliever is waiting to use: "And you call yourself a Christian."

> INFLUENCE:
> *You cannot mute words already spoken; nor is it likely you'll regret impulsive words not spoken. Silence is usually the wisest voice when frustrated. When reviled and ridiculed, Jesus answered not a word. He understood what we often do not—he who defends himself has only himself as a defender. Practical Insight: Master the art of silence by exercising it.*
> MATTHEW MAHER, 1984-

This led to an argument. It is never a good read to lose control. I could have asked them in a nicer manner to talk somewhere else or to lower their voices, but I didn't. I lost my temper and blurted out two words that spoke volumes to these men. Two words that were so legible to these men, their intensity blocked out—eclipsed—the Bible.

I apologized to the men, but the light was already snuffed. The damage was already done. On that particular day and at that exact moment, I violated the law of HIS LIGHT. I can't take my words back, but I am now even more determined to take my example back—by taking myself back to Christ in order to be HIS LIGHT.

"[...] put on the Lord Jesus Christ [...]" (Romans 13:14).

VISION RESTORED

Light makes vision possible. However, it is not the absence of darkness that constitutes light; rather, it is the presence of darkness that distinguishes light. "And the light shines in the darkness, and the darkness did not comprehend it" (John 1:5). *Your vision, therefore, should not be hindered by the darkness around you, but ought to be enhanced by the light within you. You see, to have spiritual vision is to have enlightenment in spite of tenebrous conditions. In fact, darkness is often necessary to show you how well your "I" actually sees. Do not attempt to pick your way in the dark, but let His light be your way in the dark.*
U MAY B HIS LIGHT!

Use the darkness to shine the brightest.

PART V

---

the law of HIS SEED

"Growing character is more important than showing reputation:
Character influence is seed and deep;
reputational influence is sod and surface."

appropriating the law:

Biblical influence is personal. Are you growing? Is what's inside of you showing? A developed seed is no longer a seed at all. In fact, it is something other than its original structure, from past to present. It died to its form in order to live on as its "fruit." Thus, if you are intentionally sowing to your character to cultivate the law of HIS SEED, then as a result you will perceive that you are no longer what you used to be. No longer are you just potentialities contained within a seed, but one who has birthed the fruit of the Spirit to help others in need. Remember, a seed doesn't remain just a seed. It grows character, and it shows more than reputation.
U MAY B HIS SEED!

Contrast your past with your present, and believe in the difference.

~seeing the law is being the law~

LEGIBLE

-application of the law-

"Yet I had planted you a noble vine, a seed of highest quality [...]" (Jeremiah 2:21).

When projecting the law of HIS SEED, we are to be a legible representation of the *character, conversation,* and *conduct* of Jesus Christ.

As John Bunyan said, "If my life is fruitless, it doesn't matter who praises me. And if my life is fruitful, it doesn't matter who criticizes me."

It is a noteworthy fact that for a seed to yield its crop, it must first die. It must die to itself before it can become something else. Therefore, I am to cultivate the law of HIS SEED by learning the planting process, as well as the agricultural outcome. Sowing and reaping. For if HIS SEED—the Word of God—is planted and cultivated in me, than anywhere I go I take that understanding with me. Seed *in*, fruit of the Spirit *out*. Seed *in*, strength of a tree *out*. Seed *in*, wheat of God's Word *out*. Seed *in*, greatness through humility *out*. But not first without death: *"Most assuredly, I say to you, unless a grain of wheat falls to the ground and dies, it remains alone; but if it dies, it produces much grain" (John 12:24).*

In John 12, Jesus is speaking pointedly about the person who desires to follow Him. He tells us further

> INFLUENCE:
> *Christians are not born but made.*
> JEROME, 347-420 AD

that anyone who loves his life will lose it; and for us to be HIS SEED, we must lose our life to find it. In laymen's terms, die to SELF. SELFishness. SELF-sufficiency. SELF importance. SELF-asserting. When the SELF goes, the seed grows. SEEDfulness. SEED-proficiency. SEED relevance. SEED-inserting. It is better to be seen as seedy, not needy or greedy. Let others read your seed.

Wait! Surely to be legible as HIS SEED we must be planted in a comfortable environment with every outward resource possible, right? Wrong! The first soil that matters most in this process is the soil of your heart. When HIS SEED—God's Son— is planted in your heart, Christ then becomes the only comfort and resource that one will ever need to be a good read.

In 2011, it was an unjust and abrupt move that completely caught me off-guard. No prison sojourn is nice, but the caliber of inmates can make the time more tolerable; and I had already spent 14 months of my prison term on a very comfortable and resourceful tier. On Tier 2 East, I found myself "jailing" successfully among my peers. I had everything I needed as an inmate to stay productive, and I was planted and growing as HIS SEED in this environment.

> INFLUENCE:
> *The mysterious growth of Jesus Christ in our heart is the accomplishment of God's purpose, the fruit of His grace and divine will. This fruit, as has been pointed out, forms, grows, and ripens in the succession of our duties to the present which are continually being replenished by God, so that obeying them is always the best we can do. We must offer no resistance and blindly abandon ourselves to his divine will in perfect trust.*
> JEAN-PIERRE DE CAUSSADE, 1675-1751

On Tier 2 East, another former professional athlete, NBA All-Star Jayson Williams, and I started a Bible study with one other inmate that soon included over 20 of the 38 men housed on this tier. Jayson and I were "trees" planted among our peers, and we were centered on spreading God's Word in a fresh and new way. But our influence caught the attention of the system, in a setting that sees any type of inmate influence or organization as a threat. The authorities will counter that threat in a number of punishing ways. Consequently, I was suddenly removed from the familiar and agreeable surroundings of 2 East, and thrown into soil of a completely different composition.

I was moved to a unit several tiers up in the prison, Tier 7 East, where they house the most unruly and violent inmates. Downstairs were the older, more mature and laid-back inmates who just wanted to do their time and go home. But not so upstairs. On Tier 7 East, were the wolves. The wild weeds. The gang members. In fact, every "Code 33" (a fight) that rang out in the institution came from the upstairs units—and mostly, from 7 East.

So here I was, uprooted and tossed into a very thorny field. A plot of the prison land that would choke you or poke you ("poke" means "stab" in prison) if you tried to survive on your own strength. A hard soil because of the hard mentalities—unless you know the state of your heart's soil. Unless you know the Farmer. And unless you know your role as HIS SEED.

I had a choice to make on this new tier, and I needed to make it fast, lest the weeds devour me. I don't know how I did it—actually, I take that back. I know exactly how I did it. I DIDN'T, GOD DID IT! Because I didn't want to do it. I didn't want to take root. I didn't want to be HIS SEED up there. Yet, not I, but God! I had to first decide to die to myself for God to plant me and grow me in this soil. That's the law of HIS SEED, where growing character is more important than showing reputation. Just as I had determined downstairs to be the only Bible my peers may read, so I made the same determination upstairs. I didn't know what to expect, but cultivating the law of HIS SEED leaves no room for worry. Just letting go and taking root, and watching God grow fruit.

INFLUENCE:

Success highlights deficiency. Don't be alarmed when opposition interrupts spiritual progress. Practical Insight: Set the tone of your faith early on upon entering any new setting. It's your personal conviction, so why let external persuasions to dictate it? Take root and let God produce the fruit.

MATTHEW MAHER, 1984-

I promptly started a Bible study upstairs, and it soon began to blossom. As a result of cultivating this new tier by simply opening up God's Word and sowing HIS SEED without caring about the consequences, the culture changed. Hearts were changed. And that is what being the only Bible somebody may read is all about: taking root wherever God sends you and allowing Him to sow you, water you, and eventually grow you. He will sow you as HIS SEED to be used for someone else's need!

On Tier 7 East, I was the very Bible that my peers were able to read. I was legible by the grace of God. And all because I knew God's agricultural truths. I look back in hindsight and recognize that to cultivate the law of HIS SEED, we must be willing to be planted wherever He leads us. We must know that He is the only comfort and resource that we need to rely on in any environment—in any soil, even the soil of prison.

OAK

-illustration of the law-

To cultivate the law of HIS SEED, be an oak. Be *rooted*, *reforming*, and *reliable*.

How would anyone read me as a tree? That's a good question, I'll tell you. For one, people may read you as a tree by the way you "bark" at others. But that's not a good thing. People may read you as a tree by the way you always "leave" when the going gets tough. Not a good look either. Or perhaps it could be how you "root" for others' failures and are happy when they mess up. That one's a big no-no. I could go on, but I'd rather "branch" off into a different read. One that "sticks" to the script, the Scriptures that is, by telling you how you can be a "tree of righteousness."

So since you are still reading this book and desire to be a good read yourself, I'm going to go out on a "limb" and tell you how you can be seen as an oak tree. Not just durable like the oak's wood, but enduring like the oak tree's roots.

Such Christian characteristics "stemming" from the oak tree can be the very "fell swoop" that you may need to weather the weather. What weather? Whatever the weather may be in your life that has stormed in on you unexpectedly, where your response has become

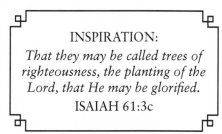

INSPIRATION:
That they may be called trees of righteousness, the planting of the Lord, that He may be glorified.
ISAIAH 61:3c

other people's forecasts—people who are watching and reading your faith.

"Let's see how they handle this situation," many may wonder, snicker, and speculate. But such looks can be a good look when your response points them to the Good Book!

No matter where you live in the world, it is inevitable that you will experience a heavy storm from time to time. Storms will come, and their level of destruction varies based on their size and intensity. They do not stop at your front door or property line because of your profession or bank account. Storms are no respecter of persons. And if the physical storms can cause so much damage, consider the spiritual and emotional storms that have the potential to ravage your soul—unless you are an oak tree and understand your roots. Not the roots of your heritage to man, which go deep, but your roots in Christ, which go deeper.

> INSPIRATION:
> *As you therefore have received Christ Jesus the Lord, so walk in Him, rooted and built up in Him and established in the faith, as you have been taught, abounding in it with thanksgiving.*
> COLOSSIANS 2:6-7

We must be rooted in the Word of God as surely as the oak tree sinks its massive root system into the earth. First, it's important to know that the oak tree's rugged sturdiness is related to the weather it has faced. Storms and high winds increase the speed of growth, resulting in deeper roots and thicker trunks. Therefore, as the tree is blown, bent and twisted, it is reformed. The integrity of the tree's wood and its firm stance in the earth is improved by the fierce hurricane that roared through. In other words, the oak tree needs resistance in order to be strengthened.

Thus, to be like an oak, we must recognize that the trials that we face "in the earth" are permitted by God to touch us in order to root us through our "hurricane happenings." Not only so that we are pushed to go deeper in our faith, but to reform and develop our integrity, our character, and our stance as HIS SEED in the earth. Remember, a tree became a tree after being a seed first.

Even an oak tree began as a mere seed planted in the world. Like you and I! I've heard it said that when God makes a mushroom, He does so overnight. But when He desires an oak, He takes years and years to nurture it. It is in the maturation process that the mighty oak is set apart from other trees and plants—and recognized for the strength of its roots, the reforming of its character, and the reliability of its substance.

> INSPIRATION:
> *Blessed is the man who trusts in the Lord, and whose hope is the Lord. For he shall be like a tree planted by the waters, which spreads out its roots by the river, and will not fear when heat comes; but its leaf will be green, and will not be anxious in the year of drought, nor will cease from yielding fruit.*
> JEREMIAH 17:7-8

Essentially, secure and powerful is what you will be, too, when you know that the storms in life aren't happening *to* you, but *for* you. For you to be an example of real faith and one that doesn't "bark" at God, but "leaves" it to God. For you to be legible as others see you standing strong like an oak tree. For you to show that whatever the weather, the Bible in you weathers the weather. The world is watching your storm coverage. How are you reporting the damage?

Be legible. Be an oak.
Be rooted. Be reformed. Be reliable.
Be the Bible!

CHARACTER STAMP:

I MAY B oak. An oak does not become an oak overnight. In fact, an oak may grow up and look formidable over time, but the roots grow down and are actually strengthened because of storms. When the powerful winds blow against the oak, the roots of the oak hold tighter thanks to those winds. We too can hold tenaciously to our strengthening and maturing faith—not based on growth that occurs chronologically, but by responding to the storms of life with trust in God firmly.
I MAY B *oak.*

Embrace resistance as the catalyst that provokes endurance.

FRUIT

-illustration of the law-

To cultivate the law of HIS SEED, be fruit. Be *bearing, bountiful*, and *beneficial*.

Be *fruit*, one who is seen as an edible and sweet product of the vine. *Jesus said, "I am the vine, you are the branches. He who abides in Me, and I in him, bears much fruit; for without Me you can do nothing" (John 15:5).* Therefore, to be read as a fruit, like a book, we must know that we are nothing without the Author. The Vine. Apart from the source, the branch withers and the fruit dies. Fruit is the product of a plant. Where is your fruit?

Being a fruit-bearer is not dependent on anything that we can do ourselves; but by sowing our spirit with HIS SEED, we will reap the Holy Spirit's fruit. Love. Joy. Peace. Patience. Kindness. Goodness. Gentleness. Faithfulness. Self-control. In other words, people will want to "pick" you! So, are you tasteful or tasteless? Bitter or better? Nutritional or artificial? Edible fruit is legible fruit. Our bounty is meant to bless others.

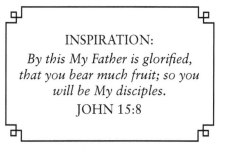

INSPIRATION:
By this My Father is glorified, that you bear much fruit; so you will be My disciples.
JOHN 15:8

It's simple! Wherever love is not, place love and love will be. Whenever joy is absent, be joy and joy will be. If ever peace is

> **INSPIRATION:**
> *But the fruit of the Spirit is love, joy, peace, longsuffering, kindness, goodness, faithfulness, gentleness, self-control. Against such there is no law.*
> GALATIANS 5:22-23

stolen, hold peace and peace will be. Whatever tests your patience, work patience and patience will be. However your kindness is taken, show kindness regardless. Whosoever questions your goodness, do goodness nonetheless. Whenever your gentleness is misunderstood, be gentleness anyway. Whatever presses your faithfulness, live faithfulness still. Though you are not in control of the situation, maintain self-control.

Such fruit can only be cultivated when you allow them to flourish in your spirit. And such favorable qualities are exactly what others will see. However, as a fruit bearer, you are also to be a fruit-starer. You are to examine the fruits of others—not with a condemning eye, but to identify. You should know whose fruit is good and whose fruit is bad, because failure to remove yourself from a "bad apple" will certainly spoil your B.U.N.C.H.: your BELIEFS, your USEFULNESS, your NAME, your CHARACTER, your HABITS.

Rotten fruit brings the flies, and "fruit flies" are watching eyes. We can become guilty—corrupted—by association, so it is important to know the state of others' fruits. And because you may be the only Bible somebody reads, where you go and with whom you associate will be the pages and chapters that you endorse. Nobody sections off space in the garden for weeds, neither would a Christian autobiography provide a chapter for pornography.

> **INSPIRATION:**
> *Even so, every good tree bears good fruit, but a bad tree bears bad fruit. [...]Therefore by their fruits you will know them.*
> MATTHEW 7:17, 20

Remember, when weeds are seen with you, HIS SEED cannot be seen in you.

Your example as a fruit-bearer will be beneficial when your presence adds antioxidants—one who builds up the inner man and keeps him from breaking down; and when you boost morale, like the vitamins in fruit that boost the immune system; and when you deliver fiber—moral fiber, that which fights the fat of perversity with integrity and cleans the stomach of pestilence with excellence.

Be fruit—and know that even when someone takes a savage bite at you, it will be your ability to swallow your pride that will result in them swallowing your virtuous vitamins. There is a saying: "Kill them with kindness"; but I say, "Feed them with fruitfulness." Let them digest your fruit that HIS SEED may come to fruition in their lives. Be a legible read by being an edible fruit.

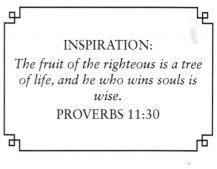

INSPIRATION:
The fruit of the righteous is a tree of life, and he who wins souls is wise.
PROVERBS 11:30

Be legible. Be fruit.
Be bearing. Be bountiful. Be beneficial.
Be the Bible!

CHARACTER STAMP:

I MAY B fruit. Fruit that may look inviting isn't always good tasting or good for you. The goodness cannot be measured by appearance or even by touch. Thus, fruit must be tried in order to discover what's inside. Sweet savor or bitter flavor? You must understand that people will try you out of love and even bite at you out of hate. For you, nonetheless, it ought not to matter why they try you—for love or hate—but whether what comes out of you is pleasing to the taste with nutritional value as the result.
I MAY B fruit.

Mind your flavor for if tasteless, praise matters not; if tasteful, criticism is no matter.

WHEAT

-illustration of the law-

To cultivate the law of HIS SEED, be wheat. Be *growing*, *gathering*, and *gleaning*.

God sows us as HIS SEED into His field, the world. But the devil sows his seeds as tares (weeds) in the world (see Matthew 13: 24-30). Essentially, believers are the wheat crop, and we grow in the field alongside the weed crooks. According to the parable that Jesus told, it is not our job to uproot the tares. No! We are to simply be aware (beware!) that they exist, planted in the same soil as we. Their goal is to take up good soil by stealing the nutrients from the ground. And they will steal from you if—and only if—you let them steal from you: your time, your energy, your peace and joy.

Therefore, just as we examine fruit, we are to look around for identification purposes, not condemnation purposes. Tares closely resemble wheat; likewise, people look like other people, and based on our limited understanding taken from appearances and surface information, we cannot properly assess another's heart. Thus, as HIS SEED and wheat planted in His field, we are instructed to grow where God plants us, that we may be gathered to Him at the harvest.

But not so fast! Being God's wheat is about growing, gathering, and gleaning on earth, so there are wheat crops that don't even know they are His yet—making your characteristics the very "grain" that must be ingrained into their "field of thought."

Treat others as if they are already in Christ!

How do the surrounding crops perceive you? Are they able to differentiate your goodness from the evil of a tare? Is your faith growing, that God's Son may grow in them? What are they gathering from your words? What are they gleaning from your actions?

Here is the "bread winner" that may help your read as HIS SEED. As wheat, you must champion the cause of Christ, making your representation of His *character*, *conduct*, and *conversation* appetizing to others. Furthermore, wheat can only produce bread and other food staples when it has undergone a gathering and grinding process. You can't rightly gather until you've been gathered!

Wheat has to be plucked or reaped; then it is cleaned to remove foreign or unsuitable seeds and contaminants. After cleaning, the wheat is conditioned (or tempered) to make it more flexible—this step is essential for creating high-quality flour. Then it is ground several times and sifted to separate particle sizes. Finally the flour is used for breads, pastas, cereals, baked goods, and as an ingredient in a host of other foods.

"And Jesus said to them, 'I am the bread of life. He who comes to Me shall never hunger, and he who believes in Me shall never thirst'" (John

6:35). So, as wheat, shouldn't our usefulness and purpose be found in Him and by Him alone? Then being the only Bible that somebody may ever read is knowing that it is only in Christ, the bread of life, that your "wheat of worthiness" finds its wholeness.

As surely as you are growing in this world, you can be certain that the pages you put out are being gathered and gleaned by others. Are you a legible or illegible harvest?

A tare's goal is to divide and conquer; but as wheat, your goal ought to be bringing people together in Christ through your wholesome qualities. Just as you are being gathered by gleaning eyes,

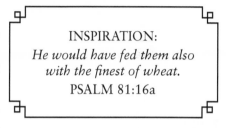

INSPIRATION:
He would have fed them also
with the finest of wheat.
PSALM 81:16a

your example's consistency is gathering their interest in God. However, without knowing your role in the body of Christ, which is to partake of the bread of life, nobody else will desire to partake either. Therefore, be Christ-like, and offer others the "breakfast of champions"® that they need in order to win in this life. It's Wheaties®, not weedies!

Be legible. Be wheat.
Be growing. Be gathering. Be gleaning.
Be the Bible!

CHARACTER STAMP:

I MAY B wheat. Wheat is an essential grain used to enrich many bread products, the staff of life. But first, the wheat must be purified and then ground into flour. Prior to that, it was nothing more than a seed that must die in order to become a grain of wheat that supplies. Thus, the wheat is spread abroad, to be used in the sustenance of health. Similarly, you must be wheat to the weak, always making the effort to strengthen the integrity of their ingredients. I MAY B wheat.

Be the ingredient that enriches quality with ingrained integrity.

MUSTARD SEED

-illustration of the law-

To cultivate the law of HIS SEED, be a mustard seed. Be *huge in humility.*

Imagine this, if you will: You are nothing more than a mustard seed among other seeds in this world. You are by far the tiniest seed—a little bigger than a grain of sand and no bigger than a grain 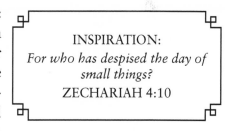 of rice. In a world that values majestic appearances, certainly nothing substantial or significant can come from such a small seed like you.

> INSPIRATION:
> *For who has despised the day of small things?*
> ZECHARIAH 4:10

Then one day, Jesus comes along and mentions you. He notices you. He references you. *"So Jesus said to them, '[I]f you have faith as a mustard seed, you will say to this mountain, "Move from here to there," and it will move; and nothing will be impossible for you'"* (Matthew 17:20).

But what did Jesus mean by "if you have faith as a mustard seed, you can move mountains"? You may wonder, "What do I, a little mustard seed, have to do with moving mountains?" And then it dawns upon you! Your internal size means everything to God. Your nucleus is what He sees—your heart. Based on the faith in your heart, your spiritual growth—your understanding, knowledge, and God-given abilities—will reach to a level

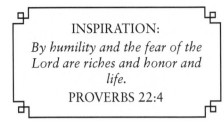

INSPIRATION:
By humility and the fear of the Lord are riches and honor and life.
PROVERBS 22:4

completely out of proportion to your size.

You are so moved by this revelation that you proclaim from your little mustard-seed stature, "Listen up! God desires that you at least have miniature faith in order to do monumental things—*not because of you, but because of Who He is!*"

I heard that little mustard seed's proclamation, and since that day I have learned that I am huge in Christ when humility is cultivated within. I am to be like a mustard seed—so small in stature, yet so large in faith. That makes me usable for God's glory.

Being a mustard seed is knowing that since Christ is on the inside of you, His clothing of humility ought to be seen on the outside of you. It's being read as someone who has submitted his life to the Lord and is content with being HIS SEED no matter where He decides to plant you—whether in a pristine penthouse or prison penitentiary.

Humility is serving in such a gentle manner that, like a mustard seed, you still remain small and lowly in heart even as your service, influence or opportunities are growing. Such meekness should point to God for His glory because we know that *we* are not of importance—rather, *God* is all that is of importance. Humility is not thinking less of yourself—it is not thinking of yourself at all.

INSPIRATION:
Yes, all of you be submissive to one another, and be clothed with humility, for "God resists the proud, but gives grace to the humble." Therefore humble yourselves under the mighty hand of God, that He may exalt you in due time, casting all your care upon Him, for He cares for you.
I PETER 5:5-7

In the seed sight of others, will you be a mustard seed for God's glory or a seed who musters up his own glory? No one is attracted to pride, except Satan. Therefore, take heed to the little mustard seed's proclamation and begin to act in faith, huge in humility. It is the language of heaven. And if it is already written up there, so it shall be down here!

Be legible. Be a mustard seed.
Be huge in humility.
Be the Bible!

CHARACTER STAMP:

I MAY B a mustard seed. A mustard seed is the smallest of all seeds, but it has the greatest proportionate growth. It produces in spite of its size, and that's what makes its relative magnitude so impressive and favorable for an illustration of faith. Thus, the monitoring of your faith's growth has nothing to do with external characteristics, and everything to with internal character.
Like the mustard seed, we must recognize the potential within, which is according to the potency of God that works through us and comes out.
I MAY B a mustard seed.

Favor follows faith, as harvesting follows sowing.

ILLEGIBLE

-violation of the law-

*"And some fell among thorns, and the thorns sprang up and
choked them" (Matthew 13:7).*

I may have begun with a time when I was legible as HIS
SEED, but there were also plenty of times when I was illegible.
It wasn't that I was just unreadable; in fact, I was inconceivable.
Clearly sterile! Thus, it is fitting that I share some examples with
you that you may learn from my choked past and do better. It
is agriculturally crucial to know every "planting principle" in
God's economy.

You see, as HIS SEED, you best believe that what He plants
will ultimately grow. However, frustrating this process is done
on our part by our stubbornness to heed His Word and feed His
seed. When we frustrate this planting process, we hinder what
God wants to accomplish in our lives. I can choke out growth
with my own hands and slash with thorns my own feet. Such
selfishness delays the growth of character according to the law
of HIS SEED.

From an early age, I knew that I was HIS SEED, a child of
God, because I was raised in a Christian household. I knew that
I had the wheat of His Word in my heart. I knew that I had the
ability to tap into oak-tree strength. I knew about the fruit of
the Spirit, and I had even memorized the Scriptural passages
pertaining to mustard-seed faith. But none of these "planting principles" could take root in my life because I was too

busy going against the grain. Knowledge without intimacy.

Intellectually knowing the law of HIS SEED in every regard does not make you legible or able to be planted in every yard. Although God's purpose for our lives can be manifested in any setting, it's important to understand that He needs us to intimately partner with Him in this farming process. This is done by cultivating our hearts and tilling our minds to make us fertile for spiritual growth; otherwise, we are sterile as HIS SEED in this earth.

> **INFLUENCE:**
> *If I am a field that contains nothing but grass-seed, I cannot produce wheat. Cutting the grass may keep it short: but I shall still produce grass and no wheat. If I want to produce wheat, the change must go deeper than the surface. I must be ploughed up and resown.*
> C. S. LEWIS, 1898-1963

This is where I went wrong: I took HIS SEED with me to inconceivable places. Situations choked out by my own hands and briar patches walked into by my own feet. I had no right to question God about "why am I not seeing growth or finding fulfillment" in this earth when I was the one taking HIS SEED into hell's bosom. If God had wanted to show His glory in my life at that time, He couldn't—because of the destruction caused by my own hands and feet, what I did and where I went, I was outside of His garden.

> **INFLUENCE:**
> *The inner life cannot be freed by changing the place or by killing the body, but only by putting off the "old person" and putting on the new person, thus passing from death to life. Those who go astray, instead of satisfying their inner craving in the Creator, try to satisfy it in their own crooked ways. The result is that, instead of being happy and satisfied, they become miserable.*
> SADHU SUNDAR SINGH, 1889-1933

I was very proactive in high school and college as far as my Christian walk would take me. But this trek usually went from the beginning point of Sunday to the ending point of Friday afternoon. And then I transferred onto another path which always led to muddy land or quicksand. Bars and clubs on Friday and Saturday nights. Then I would repeat the cycle of treading through the "good soil" of life from Sunday to Friday, only to wallow once again in dirt and get stuck in sand. God cannot grow us as HIS SEED when we are taking ourselves to places of poor and unhealthy conditions and burying His purpose for our lives.

Throughout my senior year in high school and all four years of college, I knew God and prayed to Him daily. Yet I foolishly expected Him to answer my requests and bless my endeavors when I was choking out my relationship with Him and wrapping thorns around my life. God CANNOT grow us in His Son when we are allowing the world to grow us in sin.

I made my own decision to take what is holiness (Christ) into environments of hellishness. Bars and nightclubs. Casinos and gentlemen's clubs. I made myself sterile by the places I went and the things I did, and if there was anyone watching me and attempting to read me as a Bible, my presence alone in certain settings would have been translated as a STAIN—and worse, *a stain on Christ*, and not *a Christian*.

> INFLUENCE:
> *Christ changed sinners and settings, not the other way around; yet He did not go where the Spirit could not grow. Practical Insight: Invite them to church before they invite you to the club. Exchange bar-hopping with Bible-hopping by starting your own "happy hour"—a fellowship group.*
> MATTHEW MAHER, 1984-

"*For he who sows to the flesh will of the flesh reap corruption, but he who sows to the Spirit will of the Spirit reap everlasting life*" (Galatians 5:6). I was sowing to my flesh, and even though I knew better I did not always do better. I went the way that I thought was right, and I found its end to be the way of death (Proverbs 14:12). Death to all God was trying to bless in my life.

Knowing that you are HIS SEED is not enough. In fact, when you truly know that you are carrying around His Seed, Christ, you become exceedingly careful where you take Him. I have learned deeply that God has not taken His seed away just because I choked out its fruitful effects in my life during that season. No! As stated previously, what God plants will ultimately grow in due season, but the more we frustrate these "planting principles," the more we impede the process and disrupt the harvest.

Thankfully, I have come to see the sowing and reaping process result in abundant growth in my own life. This season, in the soil of prison, I am no longer allowing my hands to choke growth nor my feet to walk in the way of thorns. It is still possible in prison to take oneself into hellish holes by hanging around hellish souls. But now I see my past for what it is, and I am determined more than ever to only nurture good soil for HIS SEED. If the background of where I allow myself to go isn't consecrated ground in which God's Word can be planted and cultivated, then I have no business being there. Certain places will never be receptive to HIS SEED no matter how you plow it up in your mind. Remember Sodom and Gomorrah—two cities that God destroyed because *"their sin [was] very grave" (Genesis 18:20-19:28).*

During that particular season and in those settings, I cared more about showing reputation than growing character. And as a result, I choked out beauty found in the law of HIS SEED. I frustrated the grace of God and made myself inconceivable. I was illegible and far from Bible. But no more!

"Do not be deceived, God is not mocked; for whatever a man sows, that he will also reap" (Galatians 6:7).

VISION RESTORED

A seed seen is not a seed sown. Therefore, in order to have clear discernment, you must be willing to be planted in isolation. The seed that will eventually be seen as a fruitful plant is the one that sets itself apart to have quality and quiet time with the Lord (private devotional time).
Spending time in the soil of isolation is the only way to gain the proper perception.
U MAY B HIS SEED!

Sow private devotion, reap public discretion.

PART VI

---

the law of HIS SHEEP

"Obedience is better than sacrifice, and practical application is more influential than theological understanding."

appropriating the law:

Biblical influence is moral. You will know you are His sheep when your "I" doesn't just know Psalm 23 by memory, but your "I" knows the Shepherd of Psalm 23 intimately. Heeding this "I" is more involved. In fact, the more our "I" becomes sheep-like, the more we evolve to be Shepherd-like. The Good Shepherd Jesus Christ leads, and your "I" follows. And when your "I" follows Him, your "I" learns to lead others as they follow you back to Him. Essentially, as sheep distinctly recognize the Shepherd's voice and follow it, so should your "I" attentively recognize God's voice and follow it. No questions asked, for obedience is better than sacrifice. Test your "I" with how well you hear—do you just read Psalm 23 or do you heed the voice of the Shepherd of Psalm 23?
U MAY B HIS SHEEP!

Check your hearing by the voice you are heeding.

~seeing the law is being the law~

LEGIBLE

-application of the law-

"I am the good shepherd, and I know My sheep, and am known by My own" (John 10:14).

When projecting the law of HIS SHEEP, we are to be a legible representation of the *character*, *conversation*, and *conduct* of Jesus Christ.

As Isaiah the prophet wrote: *"All we like sheep have gone astray; we have turned, every one, to his own way; and the Lord has laid on Him (Christ, the Good Shepherd) the iniquity of us all"* (53:6, *parenthetical emphasis added*). Thus, following the law of HIS SHEEP is knowing that God became a sheep and sacrificed Himself to pay the penalty for my sin, even though I'm the one who strayed from Him. God—Who is loving, merciful, and forgiving—is also holy, righteous, and just. He can have nothing to do with sin, and the penalty for sin is death (eternal separation from God and His goodness). Jesus took that penalty in our place, thereby restoring our relationship with God and removing the separation caused by sin.

Let's get this straight. God gave His Son to become a Man? Yes! Who then willfully became a lamb? You got it! Who then died for all mankind? That's right! So that I can live, and have life abundantly? Yes, again! And you mean to tell me this was God's plan? Correct! In order to follow the law of HIS SHEEP, you must recognize the Good Shepherd Jesus Christ as your

Leader, Provider, Protector, and Inspector. And then follow Him as such, for obedience is better than sacrifice.

> **INFLUENCE:**
>
> *When, however, we learn to listen, our lives become obedient lives. The word obedient comes from the Latin word audire, which means, "listening." A spiritual discipline is necessary in order to move slowly from an absurd to an obedient life, from a life filled with noisy worries to a life in which there is some free inner space where we can listen to our God and follow guidance.*
>
> HENRI J. M. NOUWEN, 1932-1996

Wait! Surely to be legible as HIS SHEEP we must have the whitest and purest wool, free from blemish. Wrong! Being HIS SHEEP is responding to His voice. It is not based on external beauty nor is it based on our own good works. No way!

Following the law of HIS SHEEP is coming to Jesus as you are—with all your faults and flaws, with all your sin— and never leaving His side again. But even if you do, it's knowing that the Shepherd will not give up on you; He will search for you to bring you back into His fold, no matter what. Thus, we become legible as the only Bible somebody may read when we do nothing but let the Shepherd lead. Nothing but!

It was the year 2012. That year was monumentally significant in relation to my time in prison. The arrival of this year meant that I had completed two full years as an incarcerated man of the State of New Jersey. Five months into this year, I would be given full-minimum status by the Department of Corrections. This upgrade in the security level of my classification would be granted based on various factors, but primarily because of my time progression within the system.

Full-minimum custody status is a privilege and allows an inmate to leave the prison grounds and work beyond the wall. It is also the status that makes an inmate eligible for half-way-house or halfway-back programs. It is the coveted status for all inmates; and when it presents itself to those who qualify, they most certainly take it without hesitation. It is the "Gold Membership Card."

On May 5, 2012, after serving 28 months at medium-security level, I was finally presented with the opportunity to accept full minimum and finish out the remaining 27 months of my sentence at a camp or halfway house. That change would have permitted my family to visit more frequently; and there was the possibility of passes or furloughs, which would have granted me freedom to travel in my own clothes with minor restrictions. I would still be under the jurisdiction and custody of the Department of Corrections (DOC), but my new security identification meant that I was in the final stages of my imprisonment. Having full minimum is like being on the yellow-brick road with Emerald City in clear sight, as opposed to being stuck in the Enchanted Forest and under attack by vicious winged monkeys.

Of course, it was readily apparent that family, friends, and even fellow inmates were excited for my "progressive reward"—until I turned it down and refused to leave medium security, which would leave me behind the wall. My decision echoed throughout the institution as staff and inmates alike asked, "Has Maher lost it?"

> INFLUENCE:
> *There is only one true devotion, but there are many that are false and empty. If you are unable to recognize which kind is true, you can easily be deceived and led astray by following one that is offensive and superstitious.*
> FRANCIS de SALES, 1567-1622

I was questioned by just about everyone. My refusal made no sense to the inmates, who wanted nothing more than to advance in the system's eyes. And it made even less sense to the Corrections Officers who seldom saw a person choose to stay in the midst of criminals, especially a person with a background such as mine.

INFLUENCE:

Going with God is not going against the system, it's going with wisdom. Psalm 37:23 says, "The steps of a good man are ordered by the Lord." And his stops! So whether He says, "step" or "stop," His order is always paid in full. Practical Insight: Crucial decision to make? Fast and pray about it. Fasting detaches you from the world, and praying attaches you to God.

MATTHEW MAHER, 1984-

I understood their concern and confusion, but they didn't understand my conviction. You see, I had prayed and fasted for this decision and felt strongly that my Shepherd was *"mak[ing] me to lie down in green pastures"* *(Psalm 23:2)* for another season behind the wall. It was the sincere assumption by one and all that the greener pastures lay outside the wall, but I have learned that it is possible to be sincerely wrong. The outside destination wasn't for me—not because I didn't want to go, but because God didn't say "go."

The fact that I turned down this "progressive reward" baffled my peers, and their curiosity presented me with the opportunity to open up the Bible conversationally. Whether or not they comprehended my reasoning, they most certainly left our conversations knowing that I wasn't going anywhere unless the Good Shepherd led me.

The "green pastures" He prepared for me were indeed behind the wall!

A week after I refused full-minimum status and remained behind the wall, two full-minimum inmates escaped from the unit in which I would have been housed had I accepted the offer. This pushed the DOC into action because such situations are a poor reflection on them, and because such behavior tends to give other anxious inmates an idea. As a result, the DOC shook things up by transferring all the full-minimum inmates to other institutions. In another facility, inmates must be reclassified;

and full-minimum inmates may find themselves stuck behind the wall once again.

Instead, I was left to "lie down in green pastures" exactly where the Good Shepherd wanted me. I didn't understand every single reason why I was to decline this privilege, but I felt the gentle pressure from the Good Shepherd to remain where I was behind the wall. His ways are higher than our ways, and that's why God requires practical application and obedience to His nudges, well over theologically understanding these nudges. My decision to lie down and stay put by following the law of HIS SHEEP was the "progressive reward" that made my faith legible and among my peers even more influential.

DELICATE

-illustration of the law-

To follow the law of HIS SHEEP, be delicate. Be *fragile* and *frail*.

Don't be turned off by the F words just yet! It will soon be clear why they have value. Such states of weakness in the world's eyes are very necessary in the Word's eyes. As HIS SHEEP, it is safer to be fragile and frail under the Good Shepherd's protection than bold and vigorous under your own direction. I'm not talking about walking around like you live on egg shells, but living life so that you don't break anyone else's egg shells. In other words, be seen as one who is carefully gentle and gently caring. Confidently delicate!

Sheep are fragile, frail animals by nature. They are timid and fearful; easily fooled; perversely stubborn; and vulnerable to illnesses, pests, predators, and hunger. It is through their weaknesses that the shepherd shows his strength as their overseer. He knows their frailties, so he is most effective when he leads them with calm, gentle, and loving patience even when the terrain takes them alongside raging waters or aggressive snakes. It is actually the desire of the shepherd that the sheep stay close and dependent on him.

> INSPIRATION:
> *Lord, make me to know my end, and what is the measure of my days, that I may know how frail I am.*
> PSALM 39:4

Thus, to be like a sheep, I'm not to be ashamed to refrain from going to an unstable environment just because I was invited. There is nothing wrong in staying away from the raging waters of alcohol or the snake-infested terrain of a bar or night club. There is nothing wrong with not finding humor in an off-color joke or discriminatory comment. There is nothing wrong with being sheepish and staying away from rubbish.

Being HIS SHEEP is realizing that your fragile state has you living by faith. It is your fear of the Lord and confidence in the Good Shepherd that has you being led by His wisdom and strength. **U MAY B THE ONLY BIBLE SOMEBODY READS** is not about being outwardly fractured and seemingly scared, but it is knowing inwardly that you are only safe and secure when in the refuge of the Lord, in the arms of the Good Shepherd.

Sometimes the Good Shepherd has to apply his own delicate pressure to get us to *"lie down in green pastures."* When I was offered full-minimum status in prison, I wasn't afraid to go—I was afraid to go *without consulting my Lord*. I knew that I was frail and fragile and needed His discernment. And by His gentle prompting to *"lie down,"* I exercised firm faith.

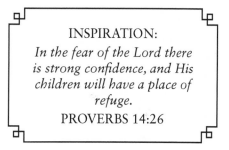

INSPIRATION:
In the fear of the Lord there is strong confidence, and His children will have a place of refuge.
PROVERBS 14:26

Failure to heed the rod and the staff of the shepherd is one of the reasons sheep go astray and get lost. Because they avoid the shepherd and his touch, they position themselves outside his help. You see, sheep may see greener pastures and go for them in spite of the shepherd's warning to lie down. Their frailties make them prone to danger.

But it is the fear of the Lord—*not fear alone*—that gives us strong confidence. Without a delicate demeanor and peaceful poise, we stubbornly move ourselves from being HIS SHEEP

INSPIRATION:

The Lord is my shepherd; I shall not want. He makes me to lie down in green pastures;He leads me beside the still waters.

PSALM 23:1-2

that *"He leads beside the still waters"* to fleecing ourselves by going near the raging waters.

Other herds will certainly read you, so how do they see you? Are you just part of the herd, going along with the crowd? Are you willful in nature? Or are you being shepHERDed by the Good Shepherd, Jesus Christ? Are you different by being delicate?

Be legible. Be delicate.
Be fragile. Be frail.
Be the Bible!

CHARACTER STAMP:

I MAY B delicate. *Sheep are delicate, easily frightened, and skittish; but their sensitivity has them place implicit trust in the shepherd. Likewise, the fears of this world ought to draw us closer in faith to the Lord. We will then hear the Words of our Shepherd: "My strength is made perfect in weakness."* **I MAY B** *delicate.*

Allow your delicacy to highlight Christ's efficiency.

DUMB

-illustration of the law-

To follow the law of HIS SHEEP, be dumb. Be *ignorant to ignorance*.

First, it's important to understand that DUMB does not have to be an insult when it is in relation to what we are being stupid about. How we apply it! Our hearts and minds should be dense to sin—closed to predators and the ways of worldly wolves and the hirelings of hatred. We should be deaf and dumb to the lurid songs of temptation.

We ought to be defenseless before the Shepherd, Who is our Defender. As HIS SHEEP, we only need to know one voice. We only need to know His familiar calls. When several shepherds gathered their flocks for the night, did you ever wonder how the sheep knew who to follow in the morning? Each shepherd had a distinct call or song that his sheep would recognize. Likewise, as HIS SHEEP, we are to be so dumb that we only know one language—one voice declaring the way, lest a hireling lead us astray. One song sang most beautifully: "*Jesus said, 'I am the way, the truth, and the life. No one comes to the Father except through Me'*" *(John 14:6).*

> INSPIRATION:
> *But I, like a deaf man, do not hear; and I am like a mute who does not open his mouth. Thus, I am like a man who does not hear, and in whose mouth is no response.*
> PSALM 38:13-14

It's that simple! I don't need to have a Ph.D., be eloquent or loquacious. No! I just need to be so dumb to the rest of the world's erudition, and elementary in knowing that there is only one truth. Then, simply follow Him.

> INSPIRATION:
>
> *And when he brings out his own sheep, he goes before them; and the sheep follow him, for they know his voice. Yet they will by no means follow a stranger, but will flee from him, for they do not know the voice of strangers. [. . .] But a hireling, he who is not the shepherd, one who does not own the sheep, sees the wolf coming and leaves the sheep and flees, and the wolf catches the sheep and scatters them. The hireling flees because he is a hireling and does not care for the sheep.*
>
> JOHN 10:4-5, 12-13

This lifestyle will absolutely bring opposition and persecution, but you can be certain the Good Shepherd will lead you *"in the paths of righteousness for His name's sake" (Psalm 23:3)*. Once on that path, like a stupid sheep that single-mindedly stays on the path because that's all it was shown and that's all it knows, so shall you only go where Jesus shows. Going this "way" by this "truth" with this "life" will incite hatred and ignorance from some, but your response is what they will take in. Thus, being ignorant to ignorance is wise!

"Then Pilate said to Him, 'Do you not hear how many things they testify against You?' But He answered him not one word, so that the governor marveled greatly" (Matthew 27: 13-14). "But He answered him not one word"! Jesus was not dumb because He didn't have an answer. No, He was being "dumb" to the question because it didn't warrant an answer. Having always spoken the truth, Jesus now chose to ignore ignorance. As HIS SHEEP, ignoring ignorance is often the wiser choice for the sake of our testimony.

Face it: Some people hate to see you do well; and given any chance, they will show off their diet of chewy gossip, beefy backbiting, and sour slandering. Such ignorance is a warning that these individuals we ought to learn to ignore—for you would not know the difference between who is a wolf and who wears wool except for the diet they reveal in conversation. Wolves in sheep's clothing may prey on your

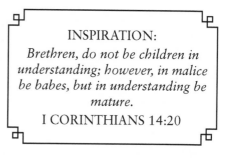

INSPIRATION:
Brethren, do not be children in understanding; however, in malice be babes, but in understanding be mature.
I CORINTHIANS 14:20

virtuous stupidity, so here is how to identify these ignorant individuals:

They may walk as sheep. Dress as a sheep. And even talk as a sheep. But how do you discover if someone is actually a ravenous wolf in sheepskin? Watch what they eat. If they eat other sheep, they're a wolf. The diet never lies—whatever is consumed by the person will eventually be produced by the person. Such ignorance is not worth your attention; instead, your stupidity lets the Good Shepherd be your validity.

Be the only Bible somebody may read by watching what you eat yourself. Only one diet can satisfy the hunger of your spirit—the Word of God. Be ignorant to ignorance by being dumb to the world's ways, the world's

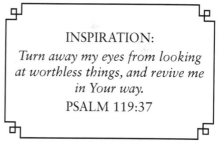

INSPIRATION:
Turn away my eyes from looking at worthless things, and revive me in Your way.
PSALM 119:37

voices, and worldly diets. That is wise and what catches eyes.

Be legible. Be dumb.
Be ignorant to ignorance.
Be the Bible!

CHARACTER STAMP:

I MAY B dumb. Sheep are dumb and easily distracted. Sometimes they are so focused on the grass below them that they can walk directly off a cliff before them. But being dumb, like sheep, to the world around us is being focused on the world above us. You must keep the goal of heaven in your sight, and this can only be accomplished by being dumb to the distractions of this world. Sheep may be stupid, but it is this type of ignorance that promotes obedience.
I MAY B *dumb.*

Stay dumb to the world to remain wise in the world.

DEPENDENT

-illustration of the law-

To follow the law of HIS SHEEP, be dependent. Be *really relying*.

We have finally come to a characteristic as HIS SHEEP that you'd expect to hear when describing a sheep; one that makes the Shepherd most gracious in giving to us, most loving in healing us, and most patient in dealing with us. Sheep are not only dumb and delicate, as we explored, but they are also extremely dependent upon their leader for survival.

The shepherd is their provider, protector, and inspector because they cannot restore themselves without really relying on him for their nutrition and sustenance; neither can they keep themselves from infections and infestations. So, the shepherd leads the sheep to places where he can feed them, while watching for predators that want to eat them. However, the Good Shepherd knows that His watchful eye is not good enough for HIS SHEEP—unless he turns it on them as well. What good is it to be an outward success, but an inward failure?

You see, the dumb sheep are unaware of the external dangers to which they are vulnerable, but the shepherd knows. He knows the dangers, and he knows their stupidity, and he knows the sheep are totally dependent upon him for security. Thus, as HIS SHEEP, we are to be really relying SOULy and fully upon the Good Shepherd Jesus. We trust Him to take care of the external dangers, and we trust Him to help us overcome the internal dangers that lust against the Spirit.

> INSPIRATION:
> *I say then: Walk in the Spirit, and you shall not fulfill the lust of the flesh. For the flesh lusts against the Spirit, and the Spirit against the flesh; and these are contrary to one another, so that you do not do the things that you wish.*
> GALATIANS 5:16-17

This is the most dependent aspect of a sheep—the process known as "inspection for protection."

That's right! Without allowing the Good Shepherd to inspect us, there can be no restoration from infection or infestation. As David wrote in Psalm 23, *"He restores my soul"* and *"He anoints my head with oil"* (vs. 3, 5). The word "restore" means to "bring back," so when we allow Jesus to bring us back to our right mind, emotions, and intellect, we are essentially allowing Him to restore our personality. Friend, it is your personality in Christ that will either attract others to your flock or repel others as they mock.

The Good Shepherd knows the condition of HIS SHEEP. When you depend fully on Him to inspect you to correct you, you can be sure He will bring you back internally while defending you against predators externally. Like sheep, we have the potential to consume poison and to have bugs burrowed in the folds of our flesh. The "bugs" of self: negativity and self-pity. The "bugs" of sin: guilt and shame. The "bugs" of Satan: depression and despair. Each "bug" is interrelated and wars against the Spirit. Each bug uses temptation and suggestion to cause infestation and infection.

The Good Shepherd knows the terrain—which plants are toxic and which are edible—and He knows the terrain of my brain and that which can be planted there to make me go insane. He desires to help us, by anointing our heads with oil. Part of the inspection process requires the shepherd to check the sheep for bugs and larvae that get into the sheep's openings. The same openings as ours—eyes, ears, mouth, nose, and pelvic cavities. There are certain parasites that can infest the sheep's brain, inducing paralysis and causing the sheep to exhibit crazy behaviors such as whirling. Though the internal issues are unseen by the human eye, the Good

> INSPIRATION:
> *Yea, though I walk through the valley of the shadow of death, I will fear no evil; for You are with me; Your rod and Your staff, they comfort me. You prepare a table before me in the presence of my enemies; You anoint my head with oil; my cup runs over.*
> PSALM 23:4-5

Shepherd will minister to us—anoint our heads with His oil. If we accept the anointing of His Holy Spirit, He will keep us free from "bugs."

For practical purposes, a shepherd would pour oil on his sheep to keep the bugs away. The oil would act as a bug repellent, preventing internal devastation. As HIS SHEEP, it is the anointing of the Spirit that will insulate our openings from the inflictions of self, sin and Satan. Such "bugs" keep us from being legible, and they make us no longer credible.

It's imperative to be really relying on our Shepherd in order to be the only Bible somebody may read. Without this SOUL dependence on Him, having the "bug" repellent from Him, there is no possible way we can win. Being HIS SHEEP is allowing Him to lead us, keep us, and feed us; but most importantly, allowing Him to read us. Let Him read you to explore you and restore you. Let Him read you to anoint you and appoint you. If you truly desire to be a good read to others, you will be dependent on the Good Shepherd's read of you!

Be legible. Be dependent.
Be really relying.
Be the Bible!

CHARACTER STAMP:

I MAY B dependent. Sheep are dependent upon the shepherd to lead them and feed them, to protect them and correct them. They can do almost nothing on their own, and this total dependence on the shepherd frees them from the pressures of the world. Similarly, your active and total dependence on God gives you total independence of mind through any situation.
I MAY B *dependent.*

Depend on God to be in-Christ-dependent.

DOCILE

-illustration of the law-

To follow the law of HIS SHEEP, be docile. Be *tractable* and *teachable.*

You must be tractable because without being easily con-trolled, you cannot be teachable to behold! To BEHOLD the goodness of the Lord. To BEHOLD the fact of faith that the Good Shepherd is always with you. And if you cannot be slowed down to be tracked down, the Lord cannot properly break you down to build you up. O, how we need this lesson to be a good read! O, how we need to be taught before we can teach.

I was often amazed that King David could write, *"Yea, though I walk through the valley of the shadow of death, I will fear no evil."* But then it became clear that he understood that as HIS SHEEP, the Good Shepherd was walking with him: *"for You are with me."* I have heard it explained that the *"valley of the shadow of death"* was a type of adversity or distressing time, and of course this can be true. But wait a second: Is it only in the "valley" of troubles that Jesus tells us not to fear? Further, is it only in the "valley" of troubles that He is with us? No! And no!

> INSPIRATION:
> *Yea, though I walk through the valley of the shadow of death, I will fear no evil; for You are with me; Your rod and Your staff, they comfort me.*
> PSALM 23:4-5

It is the overlooked reality that the *"valley of the shadow of death"* isn't just a distressing period of time on earth, but it is *all of our time on earth*. The "valley" is the earth! This passage of the Bible is telling us not to fear as we walk on this earth as living Bibles. Fear is not legible; it's fallible.

We fear no evil because when we are in Christ, we are only in the *shadow* of death—not the actuality of death. *"Jesus said, 'I am the resurrection and the life. He who believes in Me, though he may die, he shall live. And whoever lives and believes in Me shall never die. Do you believe this?'" (John 11:25-26).*

I repeat, "Do you believe this?" If you do, then you understand that death cannot devour us because Christ conquered death, leaving only its shadow to touch us. When was the last time you were hurt by a shadow? We may be afraid of shadows, but remember—a shadow can only exist because there is a light shining in the darkness.

We have nothing to fear on earth. Period. This is the *"valley of the shadow of death,"* and because the Good Shepherd took death head-on, we are only left with its shadow. I tested the fierceness of a shadow by actually standing in the shadow, or shade, of a tree. The shadow could do nothing to me. In fact, depending on your perspective and your willingness to turn your grope into hope, you can see any overwhelming shadow in your life as an opportunity to feel the cool and refreshing shade of life. Such a view will captivate "shadow stalkers"—those who watch how you walk on earth in light of death!

So if you, as HIS SHEEP, are delicate, dumb, and dependent, you become very docile. It is because of the first three D's that the fourth D, docility, keeps us from becoming hostages to hostility; kept from going astray into danger and becoming captive to animosity within and without. Here is how: Like sheep, we see our own shadow and become spooked. But instead of walking with the shepherd in the valley, we run in FEAR—(F)alse

(E)xperience (A)gainst (R)eality. We go astray out of "terrain terror." Remember, it is either the terrain of our circumstances that terrify us or the terrain of our brain that immobilizes us.

So if a sheep becomes skittish and wanders from the shepherd, the shepherd has to first find the sheep and then get the sheep under control. This is where the sheep learns to be teachable. As David wrote, "*Your rod and Your staff, they comfort me.*" These two separate tools have different purposes. The rod was used as a club for defense against predators or for disciplining wayward sheep; the staff was used for rounding up and guiding the sheep as well as extricating them from difficulties. Thus, David was saying, 'These instruments teach me not to leave Your side again, and that's where true comfort is found in the valley, in this earth."

> INSPIRATION:
> *Make me hear joy and gladness, that the bones You have broken may rejoice. [. . .] Restore to me the joy of Your salvation, and uphold me by Your generous Spirit. Then I will teach transgressors Your ways, and sinners shall be converted to You.*
> PSALM 51:8, 12-13

Spooked in the "valley"; wandering off; trouble and hostility abound. But here comes the Good Shepherd, who knows how to teach us (or chasten us) to make us reliant, really relying, on Him. You see, the Good Shepherd knows that He often has to yank the sheep back with His staff if it is veering off the path or going too close to the edge of a cliff. At times, He has to break the leg of a sheep with His rod to teach it not to run off anymore. But then He hoists the sheep on His shoulders and carries it until its leg is fully healed. Eventually, the sheep will walk again, and because of the breakdown and the intimate time spent with the Shepherd, that wandering sheep will become a wonderful sheep. Teachable by being reachable—by staff and rod. Therefore, as HIS SHEEP, we are to find true comfort in the valley that makes us contagious to others going through the valley. Everyone is looking for comfort.

> **INSPIRATION:**
> *My son, do not despise the chastening of the Lord, nor detest His correction; for whom the Lord loves He corrects, just as a father the son in whom he delights.*
> PROVERBS 3:11-12

Awareness of the valley and the shadow of death as well as the discipline of the Shepherd combine to make us docile as HIS SHEEP. When we become easily taught and led, we can then be easily read by others to reach others. That is why we walk in confidence through this valley called life—because Christ is with us, and the shadow is all that can touch us.

You're not afraid of your own shadow, are you? I didn't think so! Start helping others see the shade of faith, not the false fear of a shadow! Go for a walk today in your valley, and show others how cool and refreshing is the shade of the Good Shepherd, for He is with you.

Be legible. Be docile.
Be tractable. Be teachable.
Be the Bible!

CHARACTER STAMP:

*I MAY B docile. Sheep are easily taught, led, and managed.
They will repeatedly follow the path the shepherd has
shown them. They will habitually respond to the voice of the
shepherd or the musical notes he has played for them. This
makes them not so dumb after all—though we like sheep have
gone astray, we can learn to reweave that pattern of thought
that will bring us back to the Way. As a result, by sheep-like
docility, we express true maturity. Thus, it is the teachable
state of mind that receives more than understanding—it
receives wisdom to stand under.
I MAY B docile.*

Grade your docility by comparing it to your morality.

ILLEGIBLE

-violation of the law-

"I have gone astray like a lost sheep; seek Your servant, for I do not forget Your commandments" (Psalm 119:176).

I may have begun with a time when I was legible as HIS SHEEP, but there were plenty of times when I was illegible. It wasn't that I was just unreadable; in fact, I was unleadable. Clearly lost in translation! Thus, it is fitting that I share such examples with you that you may learn from my misleading and do better. The thought of being so illegible in my past certainly makes me ill. But such misinterpretations in my life are the translations I needed to see to find life.

I was faking it. Even though I knew the law of HIS SHEEP intellectually, I wasn't living it experientially and applying it practically. I thought that because I was gathered into the sheepfold of church each week, I was being adequately shepherded. But I have learned that you cannot claim to be following the Shepherd when you're following only yourself. The characteristic of being a lost sheep: Follow your own lead.

> INFLUENCE:
> *You can't fake real, but you can really be fake. Not only is the realest you the clearest you, but the real you is the healed you. Practical Insight: The healing of the heart begins with the healing of the past. Let God meet you there and He will take you from there.*
> MATTHEW MAHER, 1984-

I always knew I was HIS SHEEP, but I did not honor

my inner delicacy, my brilliant dumbness, my relative dependence, and my learned docility. I *knew*, but I did not *do*! To make matters even more rebellious was that I wasn't a wolf in sheepskin—no! I was a sheep in wolf skin. I put on a wolf's demeanor at times, though the sheep in me was "baaahh-h"ing. In hindsight, I know the Spirit was saying, "This is very baaahhhddd!"

I was a lost sheep, who led myself to what I believed were "green pastures"—even against wise counsel to rise up and hasten from this faux turf. Though it looked edible, it was far from digestible. Every time I led myself to this place against my sheep instincts, I was putting on my wolf suit only to devour myself.

> **INFLUENCE:**
> *If we behave like lambs, we are victorious; even though ten thousand wolves should hem us in, we survive and overcome. But if we turn ourselves into wolves, we are overcome; for the help of the shepherd is withdrawn from us. For He is the shepherd of sheep and not wolves.*
> JOHN CHRYSOSTOM, 345-407 AD

Seated at a roulette table at the Borgata Hotel and Casino in Atlantic City, finely dressed to impress, with thousands of dollars in my pocket—the grazing always began when I saw the "green grass" of green velvet in front of me. The whirling wheel with its teeth enticed me to show my own teeth, declaring, "This is no game for sheep! If you wanna win big, you had better let the wolf out." My wolf was already out and about the moment I walked onto the casino floor.

I was supposed to be there just for a nice dinner, a pleasant time with the guys, an overnight stay in a beautiful suite; but I would stray off from the group and graze on my own—enjoy my own idea of "sweet." However, this delectable meal was never a guarantee, but a gamble. So many times my friends would try to convince me not to go down to the casino floor because they knew it was a detriment to the reason we were there in the first place. My convictions would agree, but I was lost outside of myself. Beside myself. Foolishly, I would go against their guidance and feed the wolf. Funny that no matter how much I fed the wolf's appetite, I was in fact starving.

One night I sat at the roulette table with an NBA star, who was in town because his team had played against the Philadelphia 76ers. We sat at the table—attired in our jeweled accessories. Diamond bezel watches, diamond stud earrings, diamond necklaces. I remember thinking, "Anything you can do, I can do better!"

We went bet for bet, blow for blow, where initially the average chip was no less than a "black"—a $100 chip. On and on we played, as the spectators gathered round. The crowd was entertained by a roulette game they thought was for fun, but I was doing it at my own expense and might as well have had a gun. I was playing spiritual Russian roulette and taking aim at my soul.

I took the gamble to a new level. I bumped the bet up to $500 a spin and then $1,000 a spin. I challenged the NBA player—"putting the ball in his court"—but he wisely declined these ante-ups and excused himself from the roulette table. I say "wisely" now, but at the time I thought I had shamed him and felt proud about it—like I was "the man." He may have been trying to enjoy himself at this table, and I knew that. But I was a sheep in wolf's clothing and was determined to be arrogant on the outside regardless of that "baaahhh"ing on the inside.

Another time, I led myself to the green velvet grass of the roulette table to do some nibbling, but this time I bit off more than my wolf could chew. Ironically, the more I fed this false reality, the hungrier I became. I was ensnared because I led myself astray. I knew I would end up muddy and in a pig pen like the prodigal son from the Bible (Luke 15:11-31). Yet I'd still graze, only to end up lost in a maze. I have since learned that no matter how small a bite from a wolf—even just a scratch—it can still be deadly to a sheep. I was illegible as HIS SHEEP; I was perfectly legible as a wolf—faking my reality every time I went to these pastures.

This time, I began betting heavily to make up for my losses. I began at $25 on black and lost as the ball dropped on red. I then doubled to cover, but my black bet was once again beaten by red. From $25 to $50 to $100 to $200 and so forth. The roulette ball kept dropping in a red slot. I'd double up black, and it would hit red. Six times in a row. At this point, my friend Ryan strongly advised me to stop and return to the room, but I could not leave in defeat. In hindsight, leaving would have been winning—in fact, never grazing in this area would have been the ultimate victory. Nonetheless, and in spite of Ryan's constant warnings, I kept on howling!

Eventually, I tried to put down $3,200 to cover the $1,600 I had just lost, but the dealer refused to take the bet. Feeling the pressure of pride in front of the audience that had gathered once again, I split the $3,200 and tried to hit for $1,600 again just to stay in the game. As the ball spun around the wheel, I knew in my gut that I should have walked away at the first loss; further, I knew I should not even have gambled in the first place. But one nibble turned into several chews and finally a choking amount.

> **INFLUENCE:**
> *You know what happens when a portrait that has been painted on a panel becomes obliterated through external stains. The artist does not throw away the panel, but the subject of the portrait has to come and sit for it again, and then the likeness is re-drawn on the same material. Even so was it with the All-holy Son of God. He, the image of the Father, came and dwelt in our midst, in order that He might renew mankind made after Himself, and seek out His lost sheep, even as He says in the Gospel: "I came to seek and to save that which was lost."*
> ATHANASIUS, 297-373 AD

I lost close to $6,500 in that sitting, but the amount is not the point. The foolishness behind such idiotic extravagance is the point. The watchful eyes of friends and acquaintances who knew that I called myself a "Christian" outside of the casino, yet there was nothing Christ-like about me for them to see. Nothing but the wolf suit that led me, and my ego that fed me. An unleadable leader I was!

After this display, I heard about myself in a very negative way. Chatter hit the air waves about how "crazy" I was when gambling. This was far from being a dumb sheep—it was just being dumb. Clearly lost in translation.

During those grazing days in the casino, far from green pastures, I violated the law of HIS SHEEP. I was a lost sheep who put on wolfskin to unfittingly fit in. You cannot fake reality. I knew the sheep in me was starving for the provisions of the Good Shepherd. The rod was inevitable. Now, I am broken as HIS SHEEP—and wolfless for it!

"The Lord is my shepherd; I shall not want" (Psalm 23:1).

VISION RESTORED

In order to see as His sheep, you must first see yourself as His sheep and desire to be fed as His sheep. You must not worry about other sheep—or even other sheep in wolves' clothing. They will reveal themselves by their diet as well. A sheep in wolves' clothing is still a wolf and will therefore eat sheep. So focus on the Shepherd, and do not become distracted with what other people are eating. Your diet of the Word will be your clarity. Your hunger for the Word will be your consistency. And your sustenance will be your constancy.
U MAY B HIS SHEEP!

Maintain your spiritual diet by chewing on faith, and not the fat.

PART VII

---

the law of HIS CREATURE

"The unique purpose of your influence is discovered in the Source of your pulse: As felt, so follow."

appropriating the law:

Biblical influence is adaptational. Is your "I" breathing right now? From where does that breath come? It comes from your Creator and breath-Giver. God's own breath of life within you wasn't given to be taken for granted, but it was granted to claim you as His creature for living. A creature is created, thus the "I" of the creature is subject to the eye of the Creator. This law can be proved by identifying your pulse and then looking to the Source of that pulse for your influence and purpose. Breathe this truth in: Your life is from Him, making your life only breathable and adaptable in Him. Feel it, follow it.
U MAY B HIS CREATURE!

Line up your life and lips with the Spirit of life that comes from God's lips.

~seeing the law is being the law~

LEGIBLE

-application of the law-

*"Of His own will He brought us forth by the word of truth,
that we might be a kind of first fruits of His creatures"
(James 1:18).*

When projecting the law of HIS CREATURE, we are to be a legible representation of the *character, conversation,* and *conduct* of Jesus Christ.

As Martin Luther King Jr. once said, "If you can't fly, then run. If you can't run, then walk. If you can't walk, then crawl. But whatever you do, you have to keep moving forward." By whatever means you decide to move forward, know that when moving in the law of HIS CREATURE, He empowers each of us with different capabilities that faith turns into realities. With an application of the animal kingdom, we can observe and learn from the strengths of certain creatures—adopting those features to advance the Kingdom of Heaven as God's creatures. Whatever the mode of mobility: *"[T]hose who wait on the Lord shall renew their strength; they shall mount up with wings like eagles, they shall run and not be weary, they shall walk and not faint"* (Isaiah 40:31).

In this passage, Isaiah the prophet is describing the strength of the person who is nourished by God. Those who faithfully wait on the Lord are compared to an eagle and its majestic soaring capability. An eagle glides and soars as often as it can in order to conserve energy. Flapping those heavy wings takes a lot of energy, and the ability to soar enables the eagle to "go the distance" by resting on the thermal currents holding them aloft. Likewise, we can soar like eagles when we rest on the Lord—"wait on the Lord." This eagle-like attribute is ours to claim, and it doesn't stop there. As we personify many other impressive characteristics from the animal kingdom, we can be the most legible Bible somebody will ever read. And it is the Source of your pulse that births the unique purpose of your influence.

Wait! Surely to be legible as HIS CREATURE we must possess the magnificent splendor of the eagle or the royal dignity of the lion, right? Wrong! You could have the loyalty and affection of a dog, the tenderness of a dove, the adaptability of a chameleon, the unruffled serenity of a cat or even the canniness of a serpent. Being HIS CREATURE is not limited to the "top dog" or "best in show." No! Moving in the law of HIS CREATURE is exemplifying honorable attributes from across the zoological spectrum, including the most unassuming species. The work ethic of an ant. The agility of a goat. The unity of the locusts. The wiliness of a spider. It's about turning the "Animal Planet" into your animal plan for His good purpose!

Recently, I was able to tame a judgmental jackal by flapping my wings of faith. Neither Jack nor I were involved in the angry exchange that took place between two other inmates, but I knew by his cackle that he had something to say about it. His jackal cackle was a dead giveaway, so I had my arsenal of wit locked and loaded for integrity's sake.

Before the fellowship group gathered on this particular day, two of our members dismembered each other in the visible presence of the entire tier. It was a brief argument over a trivial remark spoken abrasively—which then led to a branch of insults, and the "birds" on the perch reveled in the discord.

In the jungle of prison, as it is in the world at large, those on the outside of faith are quick to point out "unchristian" behavior from those who claim to be Christians. I always find it interesting when nonbelievers set themselves up as experts on what is supposed to be considered "Christian," but I digress.

Back to the jungle with the birds' eyes who were viewing and the one jackal's mind who was judging. Moments after order was restored, the fellowship group discussed the confrontation and even moved forward with a lesson learned. The initial conflict was on display, but so was the reconciliation that followed it.

Nevertheless, in spite of the outcome, Jack the jackal said to me, "You see, that wasn't too Christian-like; was it, Matt?"

> INFLUENCE:
> *Troubles such as we are going through give opportunity to prove and to improve ourselves.*
> IGNATIUS, died circa 117 AD

Knowing his was a condescending statement meant to harm, I responded with harmony. "I know that's all that you gathered from that, but you have the Christian lifestyle all wrong, my friend." I went on to tell him, "First of all, not everyone who claims to be a Christian is one."

I also told him that being Christ-like is not about being better than everyone else or exempt from making mistakes. Rather, it's about knowing we are forgiven and allowing Christ to live through us—which slowly but surely conforms us to His *character*, *conversation*, and *conduct*. And if at any time we lose sight of the Creator, it is inevitable that we come out of character and act like unruly creatures.

I had Jack's full attention at this point, so I told him, "An individual who has Christ in their heart and lives that lifestyle can be seen in the way they suffer." Meaning, they suffer successfully. A Christian admits that he is weak; it is only in our weakness that Christ's power is perfected. It's only in our weakness that God's breath is detected. I went on and said, "When we fall, and fall we shall, a true Christian gets up and learns from their mistake to fly another day; just as you saw at the end of the dispute."

> **INFLUENCE:**
> *Do not constantly try to excuse all your mistakes. If you have made a mistake, or an oversight, or an indiscretion, confess it plainly, for virtue scorns a lie for its cover. If you are not guilty (unless it be scandalous), do not be overly concerned to change everyone's opinion about the matter. Learn to bear criticism patiently, knowing the harsh words of an enemy can be a greater motivator than the kind words of a friend.*
> JEREMY TAYLOR, 1613-1667

Jack just nodded, as I explained to him how we can even see this principle in the animal kingdom. I pointed out that the parent eagle knows this concept best, which is why the adult eagle will sometimes push an anxious eaglet out of the comfort of the nest that the unskilled bird may learn to fly through the act of falling. However, while the frightened bird is frantically tumbling, the parent is there—ready to swoop in and guard the well-being of the offspring.

Jack was now thoroughly intrigued with all that I had logically shared, so I finished flapping my wings of faith with this conclusion: "The mother eagle knows, like God, that it is only in our testing that our wings of faith can be trusted. Listen, as Christians, we never said that we are better than others who are not of our faith, rather others not of our faith say that."

Jack, who was originally a bird on the perch who relished the "air out", was now learning a Christian lesson from the birds of the air. Because of that, he now understands that there is no shame in openly cleansing ourselves from dirt in the birdbath experiences of life. Christians mess up with the best of them, but a true Christian dips himself in the water of the Word that he may suffer successfully in his failures to be an example.

The world wants our mess-ups to harm us, but the Word will use our mess-ups to harmonize us.

In the end, Jack the jackal was now Jack-back-in-his-box. After my confession that we are "no better, but forgiven," he said, "I guess you're right. And I never looked at it like that. Thank you, Matt, for taking the time to explain that to me. And for what it's worth, I listen in every day to what you guys are talking about in the group."

On that particular day and at that exact moment, I was the very explanation of the Bible that my peer needed to read. I was legible as I moved in the law of HIS CREATURE by using the animal kingdom to testify to God's kingdom. Sometimes the only way to silence a judgmental jackal is to feed him holy mackerel.

> INFLUENCE:
> *You may not convince a critic, but using God's words and ways should convict the critic. Jesus knew when to explain and when to refrain, so must we. He also was the best storyteller of all time because He knew in order to move the person spiritually; He first had to touch him emotionally. Practical Insight: Punctuate your apologetics with an anecdote or comparable parable. Interest follows intrigue.*
> MATTHEW MAHER, 1984-

BUTTERFLY

-illustration of the law-

To move in the law of HIS CREATURE, be a butterfly. Be *chrysalis-changed*.

There is natural resistance to the idea of confinement, and becoming a "Bible butterfly" has a confining chrysalis attached to it. Both butterflies and moths begin as caterpillars; but for the period of transformation, butterflies go into a *chrysalis* formed of protein while moths reside in a *cocoon* of silk. But I will explain what I mean by a "confining chrysalis" (or cocoon). First, let's talk about the main pillar in this reconstruction process—and that begins with a motley caterpillar. Knowing that you were once a motley caterpillar means that you have diverse colors and patterns, or incongruous elements, in your past, and you need not be ashamed of that. It is the change from crime to Christ that astonishes the critic. It is the transformation from addiction to conviction that amazes the skeptic. It is going from worm-like to Word-like, *being chrysalis-changed*, that makes you readable as HIS CREATURE.

> INSPIRATION:
> *Therefore if anyone is in Christ, he is a new creation; old things have passed away; behold all things have become new.*
> II CORINTHIANS 5:17

You see, though you may not want to talk about your past wormy wretchedness, the whole point of transformation is to stress a supernatural change. The word "metamorphosis" is derived from the Greek word for "transformed" or "transforming"—the very process that a caterpillar must go through in order to become a butterfly. If others see you as a butterfly, they will have a greater appreciation of your present beauty if they also have the contrasting view of your unattractive past.

Thus, being a "Bible butterfly" isn't about biologically breaking down how you've changed, but logically showing those closest to you that you've changed. It is your family, friends, and acquaintances who will see you as a new butterfly—not because they saw what happened in the "chrysalis," but because they saw you in the past as a worm.

Writing out that you have been "chrysalis-changed" for the eyes of those who know you best is indeed a hard task. Those who know you tend to think they have your DNA all figured out; so when the "new you" is living by devotion, don't be surprised when they begin to question. Even Jesus was not understood in His own hometown and by His own family (Mark 6:4). Yet, He did not waste time and energy trying to convince those neighbors and relatives who had known Him since the larval stage that He was God; He just spread His "butterfly wings" to reveal heavenly glory.

Christ is the standard; and since *He is the beauty within* us that must be revealed against the contrast of our caterpillar past, it is crucial to personally embrace your pupa stage to be chrysalis-changed. This is the transformative time when the caterpillar has its tissues broken down, and its structure is reformed. It is within the confines of the chrysalis that you are transformed, and your mind is renewed. The metamorphosis is part

> INSPIRATION:
> *And do not be conformed to this world, but be transformed by the renewing of your mind, that you may prove what is that good and acceptable and perfect will of God.*
> ROMANS 12:2

of the development process and is personally, intimately for you—and you alone!

> INSPIRATION:
>
> *Being confident of this very thing, that He who has begun a good work in you will complete it until the day of Jesus Christ.*
>
> PHILIPPIANS 1:6

When the chrysalis stage of the cycle is allowed to have its perfect way (every day), you won't need to explain what happened in the chrysalis that has enabled you to fly. No! You just fly, and your metamorphosis automatically proclaims that something supernatural happened in the chrysalis. Like the butterfly, embrace your new colors—and fly! The fact that you no longer resemble a worm will be sufficient evidence that you have been chrysalis-changed. No longer inching along, but now reaching afar. U MAY B THE ONLY BIBLE SOMEBODY READS; so let everyone see the changes in you.

We all need a chrysalis to be chrysalis-changed, but your time of confinement is individually tailored. It may be your time for daily devotionals—a time for prayer, contemplation, and Bible study. This allotted time of isolation with God alone renews your heart and mind and results in spiritual transformation. Your "confining chrysalis" is the private place where you transform into a "Bible butterfly."

Be legible. Be a butterfly.
Be chrysalis-changed.
Be the Bible!

CHARACTER STAMP:

I MAY B a butterfly. The genetic code of the butterfly was predetermined in the caterpillar, but it takes metamorphosis to bring out the transformation from immaturity to maturity, from the creeping stage of a worm to the flight of winged beauty. In a cocoon of isolation, such an excellent miracle takes place. Worm to Wonder. You may be the only Bible somebody reads, not if but when you realize you are the "beauty from ashes" they need to see (Isaiah 61:3). I MAY B a butterfly.

Wrap yourself in the cocoon of Christ, and manifest the character of Christ.

STALLION

-illustration of the law-

To move in the law of HIS CREATURE, be a stallion. Be *broken to be ridden.*

Quiet confidence. Strength under control. Brilliant poise. Calm courage. Bridled power. Usable is rideable. And rideable is readable. You are a stallion when you know you are broken and better for it! Being broken is what separates a prestigious gentleman from a purpose-driven *gentle*-man.

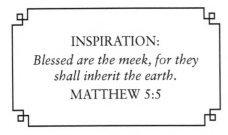

INSPIRATION:
Blessed are the meek, for they shall inherit the earth.
MATTHEW 5:5

When a stallion, act like a stallion. You know you're a stallion—not because of your physical breed, but because of your spiritual steed. It has nothing to do with your greatness and everything to do with your meekness. Meekness is not weakness—it is power under restraint. Your *horse power* is harnessed by *Holy Spirit power*! For your horse race to be worth watching, it must be paced by grace.

The Greek word for meek is "praus," which literally describes a wild horse tamed to the bridle and therefore denotes a powerful stallion broken and able to be ridden. The stallion still possesses its strength, but it is now gentle and poised and able to be used. Hence, a person who is meek possesses a gentle strength about him, a humble outfit upon him, and a usable spirit within him.

Stallions are male horses, so this is my "call out" for the men to mount up (or man up) in this perverse generation— my way of reminding the men to be leaders. The head and not the tail. Bridled by the Bible. Too often, we men spend more time and energy trying to establish our reputations for being gentlemen of renown. However, when we strive to be a meek or humble man, we become more than just a gentleman of reputation—we become a *gentle*-man of character. A stallion!

> INSPIRATION:
> *Who is wise and understanding among you? Let him show by good conduct that his works are done in the meekness of wisdom.*
> JAMES 3:13

A stallion is no longer wild in the world, but broken in the Word. A horse that others choose for its bearing and manners, not one that is always horsing around and causing trouble. You can be legible as a gentleman, a rider or performer in relation to equestrian competitions. Or you can be legible as a *gentle*-man, a Christian in relation to stallions. There is a difference.

You can be a gentleman by setting a trendy pace, but only a *gentle*-man knows he is what he is purely by God's grace. A gentleman strives to leave a lasting impression for fame, but a *gentle*-man makes known that his progression is accomplished only in Jesus' name. A gentleman leads and looks to be served, but a *gentle*-man serves by looking for who is in need. A gentleman will do what he has to do just

> INSPIRATION:
> *Come to Me, all you who labor and are heavy laden, and I will give you rest. Take My yoke upon you and learn from Me, for I am gentle and lowly in heart, and you will find rest for your souls. For My yoke is easy and My burden is light.*
> MATTHEW 11:28-30

to go the distance, but a *gentle*-man is not bound by a measure or length—just persistence. A gentleman wants the respect of others, but a *gentle*-man gives respect to others.

The differences are many, but the separation is only one. A gentleman follows other men's examples, but a *gentle*-man follows the example of only One—Jesus is that *Gentle*-man.

Be legible. Be a stallion.
Be broken to be ridden.
Be the Bible!

CHARACTER STAMP:

I MAY B a stallion. A quote from Star Trek (2009) states: "A stallion must first be broken before it can reach its potential." A stallion that is harnessed is "horse power" channeled for service. The Greek word for "meek" is "praus," which conveys more than mildness and gentleness; it actually depicts the scenario of a broken stallion—the blend of gentleness and strength. Therefore, like a stallion, a meek man is not a weak man. He is a man with God's strength under God's control. I MAY B a stallion.

Let your poise be your power.

ANT

-illustration of the law-

To move in the law of HIS CREATURE, be an ant. Be *industrious, intentional,* and *incredible.*

I could tell you to be like my older brother, Ant, which would indeed be a good thing—but that's not the ant I'm talking about. The one we need to be like is the insect that exemplifies within its species an impeccable display of social order and diligence. Not only are ants socially incredible, they are individually incredible.

You may not have thought you could learn from an insect. But even King Solomon wrote about the intelligence and diligence of ants. Inspired by God, the king instructed the idle loafer to gain wisdom from observing the ways of the ant (Proverbs 6:6-8). The lessons for mankind from this tiny, insignificant creature would make us significantly wise as HIS CREATURE.

Upon studying ants, one would learn that they have no captain or ruler, yet they work in harmony for a very intentional purpose. They store up all their food in summer in order to have provisions in winter. Thus, to be like an ant in this regard, one must know that every season matters.

INSPIRATION:
Go to the ant, you sluggard! Consider her ways and be wise, which, having no captain, overseer or ruler, provides her supplies in the summer, and gathers her food in the harvest.
PROVERBS 6:6-8

You cannot disregard the possibility of a dry or barren time—a season of drought or deprivation—so it is important for you to make each day count with an industrious attitude. Like the ant, your effort must not fall short of those around you, thereby increasing their burdens.

Wherever your workplace may be, your co-workers will be watching the level of your labor. Red flags that may fly over your ant hole, and turn others away from your Christian *anthem*, will be attitudes such as greed and selfish ambition or the opposite—laziness and self-indulgence. How is your work ethic affecting others?

You may have seen an ant carrying a crumb from a picnic blanket. That crumb is the ant's cross to bear. Typically, ants carry objects that are 10-to-50 times their body weight; weaver ants can carry up to 100 times their body weight. This would be like a 220-pound man lifting 11 tons over his head—or, like watching him walk out of a restaurant carrying the entire buffet bar on his back. "That's incredible!" we would exclaim, but we see the ant accomplish this task over and over again. Does the sight inspire awe in the abilities of this little creature?

> INSPIRATION:
> *But God forbid that I should boast except in the cross of our Lord Jesus Christ [...].*
> GALATIANS 6:14

We are not asked to carry objects 10 or 50 or 100 times our body weight; but we must frequently carry emotional burdens that seem to weigh as much. To be incredible in the ant-like way, we do not carry those burdens in our own strength—but by our faith in God, Who is our only strength. Carrying our crosses gracefully is the *anti*thesis to anything anti-Christ.

When we bear our crosses successfully, we are doing so with the purpose of being pro-Christ. When the ants are heaving their crosses with such intensity and persistence, they do so because they act instinctively for their part in the community. So, like the ant, we carry our crosses willingly to help others redemptively.

That brings me back to the ant's characteristic of being intentional when working. The ants work with deliberation, never losing track of their desired goal as social players (or cross bearers). So shall your work ethic be as the only Bible your co-workers may read: intentionally legible.

When you know you are being observed, even by ant-eaters, you are prepared for anything that comes your way and are able to handle it accordingly. When *antag*-onized, you don't respond irrationally—like you have ants in your pants.

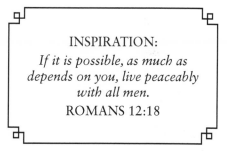

INSPIRATION:
If it is possible, as much as depends on you, live peaceably with all men.
ROMANS 12:18

No! You know you have the *anti*dote to hostility—hospitality; and by your spiritual *ant*enna, you will be wise enough to intentionally hold your peace to live peaceably.

Make your co-workers respond in awe, "That's incredible," by the way you bear your cross. Remain diligent in God's grace, realizing that anteaters want to devour you and consume your faith. Go to the ant and learn her ways that you may give God all the praise—in season and out of season.

Be legible. Be an ant.
Be industrious. Be intentional. Be incredible.
Be the Bible!

CHARACTER STAMP:

I MAY B an ant. An ant may look ordinary and insignificant, but its work ethic is significant and extraordinary. Like an ant, you must recognize that wisdom is justified by its behavior. For wisdom in your labor, your work ethic will begin with your Word ethic.
I MAY B an ant.

Work to add the "extra" to the ordinary.

DOVE

-illustration of the law-

To move in the law of HIS CREATURE, be a dove. Be *love compelling*, *peace propelling*, and *dirt repelling*.

The dove with its beautiful whiteness represents purity, which is the very reason the Holy Spirit is depicted as a dove in Scriptures. The harmlessness of the dove makes it the physical emblem of the Holy Spirit, also called the gentle Helper and great Comforter. "*[Jesus] saw the Sprit of God descending like a dove and alighting upon Him*" *(Matthew 3:16).*

Can we be dove-like ourselves? Can we partner with the Lord's Dove from above and be seen as one here below by our love? In learning about the dove, I found some very

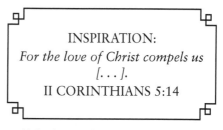

INSPIRATION:
For the love of Christ compels us [. . .].
II CORINTHIANS 5:14

interesting characteristics that will help us be legible as doves and display our love. Dove love.

Throughout this section, moving in the law of HIS CREA-TURE has been "eye" specific. As a butterfly, it is for those eyes who knew us as worms, people who knew us in the past. As a stallion, it is a call to men that they "man up," and be a *gentle*-man. As an ant, it is for the eyes of our associates or co-workers. Thus, being like the dove is specific for your re-lationship—the eyes that will observe you and your marriage partner. Can your relationship be seen as a dove, and not just love?

The dove is the world-wide symbol of peace. Peace in a relationship doesn't mean there will be an absence of problems, but an absence of tension and chaos. Thus, to be like the dove, we are to leave people or places that may cause fighting or stir agitation in our relationships. Unlike vultures, crows, pigeons, blue jays, and other notably aggressive birds, the dove rarely fights and is known instead for being affectionate. Have you done everything possible to replace fighting with affection? If you have, I believe the bird-watching world will see peace in your relationship.

Additionally, the dove is one of the few creatures that mates for life. The faithfulness of the dove is love compelling. Furthermore, the dove has "powder feathers" that produce a fine, water-resistant powder that keeps the bird clean. Likewise, does your relationship keep itself clean by its feathers of fidelity? Are you repelling dirt with prayer? Are you spiritually yoked together with a believer? Are you bonded by the Bible?

The most effective evangelism tool that we can use to bring the Bible to life is in our relationships and by our behavior displayed in those relationships. If our love, peace, and purity can write out to the world that we are dovish and not devilish, then they may want the "bond of perfection" that we have. Are we personifying the qualities that attractively pull others to Jesus or aggressively push them away?

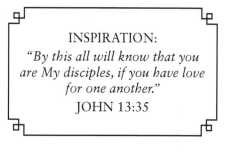

INSPIRATION:
"By this all will know that you are My disciples, if you have love for one another."
JOHN 13:35

Be legible. Be a dove.
Be love compelling. Be peace propelling. Be dirt repelling.
Be the Bible!

CHARACTER STAMP:

I MAY B a dove. Being dove-like is being love-like. Pure. Gentle. Doves have dirt-repelling features so even if they find themselves amidst dirt and muck, such conditions do not taint them. As if they were sanctified by the Good Book, they never lose their clean look. You are such a dove when you learn to put on holiness from above. Remaining sure of your internal sanctification is your outer "dirt repellent" that keeps you from the world's putrefaction.
I MAY B a dove.

Evoke sanctity by fostering Christ-identity.

ILLEGIBLE

-violation of the law-

"And there is no creature hidden from His sight, but all things are naked and open to the eyes of Him to whom we must give account" (Hebrews 4:13).

I may have begun with a time when I was legible as HIS CREATURE, but there were plenty of times when I was illegible. It wasn't that I was just unreadable; in fact, I was hypocritical. Clearly masquerading! Thus, it is fitting that I share such examples with you that you may learn from my many masks and do better. The word "hypocrite" comes from the Greek word *hupokrites* which means "one who wears a mask, or mask wearer."

Behind this definition is the idea that a hypocrite was an actor, a dissembler, one who assumed a character, a phony. In ancient Greek culture, actors were called *hupokrites* for their theatrical performances. They wore exaggerated masks to express various emotions—large smiles, sad frowns, furrowed brows—that were large enough to be seen by the audience members who sat in the farthest seats from the stage. From the Greek *hupokrites*, we get the negative connotation of a person who is "two-faced"—one who is insincere and deceitful, and likely to turn on you.

Masquerade balls became popular throughout Europe during the Middle Ages. These festivities were usually hosted by nobility or held publicly in association with carnivals. Attendees wore masks and sometimes costumes to conceal their true identities. Hidden behind the masks, men and women often engaged in improper behavior.

The bare face can reveal so much, and based on the history of the mask, I clearly see my own hypocritical ways. You see, many times I showed myself as a hypocrite, concealing my true face where the masquerade was any social gathering of my choice. I blended right into the setting, like the chameleon that can change color to fit into its surroundings. Whatever character I needed to be, I was talented enough to put on that mask and express that emotion. Gallant leader. Cold brawler. Rowdy partier. Serious scholar. Dedicated athlete. Considerate escort. Yes, even a "good" Christian. In any setting, under any conditions, I was able to wear that particular mask. Not just wear it, master it. I was a hypocrite in the fullest sense of the word.

> INFLUENCE:
> *The terrible thing, the almost impossible thing, is to hand over your whole self—all your wishes and precautions—to Christ. But it is far easier than what we are trying to do instead. For what we are trying to do is to remain what we call "ourselves," to keep personal happiness as our great aim in life, and yet at the same time be "good." We are all trying to let our mind and heart go their own way—centered on money or pleasure or ambition—and hoping, in spite of this, to behave honestly and chastely and humbly. And that is what Christ warned us you could not do.*
> C. S. LEWIS, 1898-1963

Until my senior year of high school, I was a "face wearer," not a mask wearer. Up until that time, I had a deep faith and an active witness for the Lord. I was the president of our Bible Club in my public high school. This was not a façade because I was comfortable with my identity and who I was.

I was a standout athlete and student, but I also stood for my convictions and my faith. Everyone knew this about me, whether or not they believed it about me. I knew who I was

> INFLUENCE:
>
> *My first and chosen name is Christian. But if you are asking for my name in the world, then I call myself Carpus.*
>
> CARPUS

in Christ at that age. But then something happened as I entered my senior year. I went from moving in the law HIS CREATURE—a "biblical chameleon," a strong Christian with the ability to learn quickly and adapt in any situation for His glory—to my own creature, a hypocritical chameleon with the ability to learn and adapt in any situation for my own glory. What happened? I was still a standout athlete, a straight-A student, at the top of many extracurricular activities, and still Bible Club president.

But I drank alcohol for the first time as a senior. From this poor decision, masks developed that falsified my true face and my true personality. The more I drank at parties, the more masquerading I entertained. Soon, certain masks from certain social gatherings were being worn on a daily basis. I learned that, while I thought I was pretending, it was impossible to wear an identity without becoming that identity.

As word spread about me—as a drinker, and then the alcohol-related stories—I realized that I had substituted my truth for a counterfeit mask. The new reputation I was developing felt fraudulent, but its ruinous effects were all too real. Yet, I still continued in my chameleon ways, as if I could hide; but even if others didn't see, God saw. He always sees us completely bare of cover and camouflage. But I wasn't thinking about that then; I thought I was just enjoying life.

Being Bible Club president for the second year in a row was a legible position among my peers that my actions outside of school made illegible. All of this "mask wearing" was finally disclosed at the homecoming dance. Foolishly, I decided to drink alcohol before going to the dance. I was then caught drinking at the dance, and the result was suspension from school. Worse, my example as Bible Club president was harmed, and my un-masked face revealed a hypocrite.

In hindsight, the many masks in my past kept me from being used and read as HIS CREATURE. It is im-possible to find your unique purpose in life from the Breath of Life when you're wearing a suffocating mask. Thus, I have come to learn that there is never any peace in wear-ing masks. There is never any comfort in faking truth. There

> INFLUENCE:
> *Wearing multiple faces causes onlookers to squint in confusion, and it also gives you double vision. And if you cannot see clearly, then you cannot lead confidently. Practical Insight: Take down the masks, learn to wear more hats.*
> MATTHEW MAHER, 1984-

is no hope in false living. Thankfully, my identity has never been more confident than it is today—and all because I wear one face. My face, covered by the blood of Christ. His perfect work on the cross covers my life, and now I seek to only reveal His *character*, *conduct*, and *conversation*.

During that particular season and at that exact moment, I vi-olated the law of HIS CREATURE. I was the master of my own masquerade that allowed pride to have its wretched way. I was hopeless. And without hope in the future, there is no purpose in the present.

"For what is the hope of a hypocrite [...]" (Job 27:8).

VISION RESTORED

Most creatures have multiple eyes in order to detect both direction and distance. But to see clearly with your heart's single "I," you need not worry about other creatures' eyes staring back at you; instead, trust that it's God's eyes that are watching the back of you. "For the eyes of the Lord run to and fro throughout the whole earth, to show Himself strong on behalf of those whose heart is loyal to Him " (II Chronicles 16:9). *Thus, perfecting His vision is giving your "I" faithfully to the Lord for His might to be your sight.*
U MAY B HIS CREATURE!

When your heart looks up to Him, His strong hand looks out for you.

PART VIII

---

the law of HIS VESSEL

"The content you're carrying is the intent of your influence:
As within, so without."

appropriating the law:

Biblical influence is intentional. Fulfilling this law has
nothing to do with looking at the letters on the eye-chart
and everything to do with knowing the letters on your
heart-chart. It is understanding that you may be the only
Bible somebody reads, and the basis of how they read you
is dependent upon what comes out of you. Fresh water and
bitter water cannot come out of the same vessel at the same
time. Neither can the Good News of Jesus Christ be spread
simultaneously with gossip, lies, cursing, and negativity.
What comes out is what others will believe you are about.
Thus, becoming aWARE of what you are about is knowing
that the content you're carrying is the intent of your
influence: As within, so without.
U MAY B HIS VESSEL!

Examine your heart with the evidence found on your
tongue.

~seeing the law is being the law~

LEGIBLE

-application of the law-

"But the Lord said to him, 'Go for he is a chosen vessel of Mine to bear My name [...]'" (Acts 9:15).

When projecting the law of HIS VESSEL, we are to be a legible representation of the *character*, *conduct*, and *conversation* of Jesus Christ.

I like to say that whatever you fill yourself up with will eventually spill out. As within, so without. Thus, to fulfill the law of HIS VESSEL on earth, we are to carry the contents of Christ, the "treasure" of Christ, which is the power of God. To understand better what it is to fulfill the law of HIS VESSEL, consider the words of the Apostle Paul: *"But we have this treasure in earthen vessels, that the excellence of the power may be of God and not of us"* (II Corinthians 4:7).

"Earthen vessel" in this passage means "clay pot." It was common practice in ancient times to bury treasure or other valuables inside of clay jars. In the days before bank accounts, such "safety-deposit boxes" were best kept buried in the dirt of your back yard. Likewise, it is the verse's implication that we are clay jars, and the treasure of Christ indwells our earthly bodies. Ultimately, His heavenliness will be seen in comparison to our earthliness.

Wait! Surely to be legible as HIS VESSEL, we must be as lovely in appearance as a golden chalice or as solid in structure as a great ship, right? Wrong! Those clay pots were as standard and ordinary as cardboard is today. They were common, cheap, breakable, and disposable. Like the clay jars formed by the potter from the dirt of the ground and destined to hold treasure, we too have been formed by the Potter from the dirt of the ground and destined to hold treasure—the beauty of Christ, the excellence of the Holy Spirit, the love of God. Being HIS VESSEL is knowing your composition is made of dirt so that your life can have direction in Christ. Being HIS VESSEL is personifying the container that bears His Word for ministry. Ultimately, it is allowing the "pages" within your "book" to speak the title on your "cover" with clarity, consistency, and constancy: the Holy Bible!

As I write this book from prison, I realize anew each and every morning that I am HIS VESSEL in this place. His cup. Becoming an inmate of the State, wearing these clay-colored prison garbs, has not replaced my Christian identity of conviction or my athletically driven identity of commitment. I now know that both disciplines have intertwined and enabled me to become the vessel God requires—I am His "clay-jar inmate."

Before I even allow my feet to hit the floor, I have learned how the pouring out of God's anointing must be received while on my knees and under His spout. I literally roll out of my bunk to the floor at 5 A.M., turning my bed into an altar and my heart and mind into a cup. This literal "rolling" becomes a mental and spiritual filling before I can spill out onto my day and my peers effectively. Intentionally.

From there, I proceed to one of the tables on the tier to fill up some more through my devotionals and the reading of God's Word. It has been obvious to me that this early morning commitment, spanning three hours from 5 to 8, is the only reason I am able to fulfill the law of HIS VESSEL in prison.

Isolation before interaction is necessary. There is much perversity and even more immorality spewed out relentlessly. It can easily be forced upon you or absorbed by you without your conscious awareness through vulgar jokes, pornography, lewd remarks. Unless you are already filled up with the right "substance" and have an appetite for righteousness as HIS VESSEL, you may allow yourself to be filled with filth. I have learned that my daily commitment has been an opportunity to show the

> INFLUENCE:
> *Be an example to all of denying yourself and taking up your cross daily. Let others see that you are not interested in any pleasure that does not bring you nearer to God, nor regard any pain which does. Let them see that you simply aim at pleasing God in everything. Let the language of your heart sing out with regard to pleasure or pain, riches, or poverty, honor or dishonor, "All's alike to me, so I in my Lord may love and die!"*
> JOHN WESLEY, 1703-1791

other inmates that my example throughout the day is only as Christ-like as the time I spend having breakfast with Christ.

From 6:30 to 7 every morning, my peers pass by on their way off the tier to the cafeteria. They wonder aloud why I don't join them for breakfast. One morning, from his place in the line of over 30 inmates waiting for the gate to open, Swirl asked, "Why do you never eat in the morning?"

I replied, "I am eating." I smiled my way back to my readings. My short response was enough to whet his appetite to find out what I meant.

When Swirl came back from the mess hall with his cup of coffee, he asked, "Why don't you at least go down for coffee?"

I told him, "My devotional time is my food and drink, and sacrificing this time in the AM is the only way I am able to be effective and efficient during the day."

Swirl looked bewildered. After a moment, he gave a verbal shrug. "I guess," he said, and then walked away.

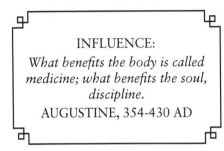

INFLUENCE:
What benefits the body is called medicine; what benefits the soul, discipline.
AUGUSTINE, 354-430 AD

After a while, however, Swirl and the rest of my peers began to see my consistency as it pertained to my "breakfast filling." Whether they understood it or not, the constancy of the AM commitment was the source of my apparent clarity for the PM pressures that normally destroyed peace and joy for everyone else.

Morning after morning, the inmates returned from the mess hall with their cups filled with coffee or milk. Their cups were soon empty. Meanwhile, my "cup" was still being filled. The law of HIS VESSEL was being fulfilled. Being the only Bible my peers may read required me to be the Bible they would read before going to breakfast. I knew the only possible way for my words and actions to point directly to Jesus throughout the rest of my day was to give up the time it took to enjoy breakfast and use that time instead to break-fast with the Lord. Instead of bringing my cup down to the chow hall for coffee, milk or juice, I brought my "cup" (myself) to the Lord for the filling of His substance. HIS VESSEL for filling and eventual spilling.

It has been my morning breakfast with Jesus that has enabled me to be the Bible to my peers in this environment. As I take a look at my own "pages," which I endorse in my conversation, and my own "pictures," which I claim in my conduct, I must ask myself if I'm allowing Christ's character to be seen in my "book cover."

Telling others what the Bible says is a whole lot different from showing them what the Bible says in our actions. So from days to months to years, it has been my desire to begin each day under His spout—filling up and spilling out. Remember, the content you're carrying is the intent of your influence. On these particular days and at those exact moments, I was the very Bible my peers were able to read. And all because the filling came from God's Word and the spilling pointed back to God's Son. I never knew exactly what the days would hold, with fights and

> INFLUENCE:
> *Your spiritual disciplines are faith strongholds. Let Christ's strength hold your heart, which creates good habits and fortifies your home. Heart. Habits. Home. Practical Insight: Carve out space every AM and/or PM for devotional time. It's only a commitment if it's consistent.*
> MATTHEW MAHER, 1984-

shake-downs and chaos, but being the only Bible somebody may read is about trusting God—the One Who knows exactly what each day holds. He will fill you as HIS VESSEL if you are willing to be poured out for His glory. And that's the intention within the law of HIS VESSEL.

CLAY POTTERY

-illustration of the law-

To fulfill the law of HIS VESSEL, be clay pottery. Be *in the Potter's hands to be in the Potter's plans.*

INSPIRATION:
But now, O Lord, You are our Father; we are the clay, and You are our potter; and all we are the work of Your hands.
ISAIAH 64:8

No matter your mar and no matter your scar, when you are clay, the Potter will reform you for His intended purpose. But first, you must submit to the Potter's wheel—knowing that to be in His plans, you must commit yourself to His hands. Often in life, we so desire to be displayed as the finished product, but we are unwilling to go through the process. It should be the opposite. We should desire to go through the process, knowing that God is willing to display us as the finished product.

However, before God can endorse, He must reinforce. Sometimes through throwing and pressing, sometimes through pounding and rolling, sometimes through spinning and shaping—but always, we are in His hands. God knows that sometimes imperfections can be hidden in the clay, so He puts us through the pottery process to rid us of such mars and smooth out such scars. For instance, the potter knows that unless air pockets, called "holes," are eliminated, the pottery will not be able to withstand the heat of the kiln—it will literally explode. So, with each slap and rotation and twist and pinch,

God is molding us through our circumstances to bring us into acknowledgment of His loving work in our lives.

You may feel that the world around you is pounding on you and pointing out your "sticks and stones"; but if you are surrendered to God, then you can be sure you are in His hands even when you can't see His plans. And His hands will always repair the mar and bring purpose to the scar.

Eventually you will make it to His wheel for forming, which is why it is important to identify your "wheel." Your wheel is the time you spend in the Word, placing the clay of your being—your mind, body, and spirit—into God's hands. Like the clay on the potter's wheel, you will be in position for God to conform you to His Son's image no matter what your outward circumstances may be.

> INSPIRATION:
> *The word which came to Jeremiah from the Lord, saying: "Arise and go down to the potter's house, and there I will cause you to hear My words." Then I went down to the potter's house, and there he was, making something at the wheel. And the vessel that he made of clay was marred in the hand of the potter; so he made it again into another vessel, as it seemed good to the potter to make. Then the word of the Lord came to me, saying: "O house of Israel, can I not do with you as this potter?" says the Lord. "Look, as the clay is in the potter's hand, so are you in My hand, O house of Israel!"*
> JEREMIAH 18:1-6

Therefore, being the only Bible somebody may read is knowing that consumers will be watching this process through the shop's window. They will watch, not out of concern for what you're going through, but only to see if you will get through what you're going through.

Truth be told, the window shopper only wants to see the finished product and whether or not it's usable. The clay pottery enthusiasts will only care about your purpose. Are you able to hold what they pour into you? Can they confide in you and rely on you? Will they recognize the hands that formed you through your personality formation? And will the product of your character wear the label of your Potter?

Here is the secret quality of your clay. As clay is molded into a vessel, the ultimate use of the vessel depends on the part where nothing exists: the inside of the vessel. Thus, when the inside of you as "clay pottery" is open for Christ to turn your nothingness into substance, then your "clay pottery" becomes beautiful to behold and able to be sold!

> INSPIRATION:
> *For He knows our frame; He remembers that we are dust.*
> PSALM 103:14

Consumers may scrutinize you with their eyes to make sure their purchase—their decision to buy into your product—has usefulness. Why will others desire your "clay pottery" if your mar or scar is all they see? Why would they buy into your faith if all they hear from you is fretting over your faults, flaws, and fractures? Your exterior display should always represent your Potter's interior molding. It is only in His hands that He begins to unfold your personality as a usable quality that attracts others to His pottery.

Without surrendering to your "wheel," there can be no appeal. The idea behind allowing God the Father to form you as clay is acceptance that He knows what is within us that needs to be pulled out of us. He does not create us and work on us to keep us on the shelf as "clay pottery." No! He wants us to be reliable products for the benefit of those nonbelievers who will look to buy into our physical, mental, and spiritual formation. In the same way the world sells its products, you need to realize that you are selling your product of clay pottery to the world. Can you sell your faith by living your faith? Does your label—your formation—say, "Made in the Potter's House"?

Be legible. Be clay pottery.
Be in the Potter's hands to be in the Potter's plans.
Be the Bible!

CHARACTER STAMP:

I MAY B *clay pottery. "Sincere" literally means "without wax" and comes from the example of inferior pottery that had been mixed with wax by unscrupulous potters. The wax would be exposed when the pot melted in the sun. Therefore, sincere pottery can hold its contents successfully, even through blistering trials. Be the sincere clay pottery that does not melt under pressure. Suffer successfully, and hold the substance of your faith confidently.*
I MAY B *clay pottery.*

Reinforce your clay by remaining in the Rock, Jesus Christ.

TEMPLE

-illustration of the law-

To fulfill the law of HIS VESSEL, be a temple. Be *orderly*, *offering*, and *officiating*.

A temple is HIS VESSEL in the same way that the heart pumps blood through 60,000 miles of blood vessels. In the same way, countless "temples" make up the body of Christ from Whom flows life by His blood. Essentially, each member plays a part in the whole—the body of Christ—and I'm not talking about a structure or organization. Rather, a living organism. Thus, being a "temple" is knowing that your body, as a temple for the indwelling of the Holy Spirit, now becomes a walking and talking church. A believing and breathing chapel. A living and giving sanctuary.

As a temple, everywhere you go, you are taking your church building with you. As your exterior is groomed and manicured, do not forget that the most attractive part of your temple must be the interior—and what's inside will always come out.

INSPIRATION:
Or do you not know that your body is the temple of the Holy Spirit who is in you, whom you have from God, and you are not your own?
I CORINTHIANS 6:19

Pews, altar, pulpit, choir loft. Do people feel safe in your presence—sheltered from danger or trouble? Will those who do not know your "doctrine" still sit in your "pews" and feel welcome? Are you always ready with a word to share from the pulpit of your heart? Like an altar, will people find you open to their burdens, problems or requests? Is your disposition inviting or frightening?

Being like a temple is carrying yourself in such an orderly way that those who see you will indeed feel drawn to rest in your "pews" because they want what you have. Your conduct is not just nice, it's flavored like the incense of spice. Your character

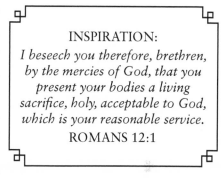

INSPIRATION:

I beseech you therefore, brethren, by the mercies of God, that you present your bodies a living sacrifice, holy, acceptable to God, which is your reasonable service.

ROMANS 12:1

is not just warmed by the blood, it's formed by the blood. And your conversation is not just church-acceptable, it's Christ-legible. When you have their attention—not through pomp of self, but on point with Christ—you can begin with the offering. No, not *taking from* them, but by *offering yourself to serve* them.

As a walking and talking temple, you must place the offering plate on the ground each day and humbly step into it. Then, having given yourself to God, your prayer is, "Lord, lead me where You need me today!" You can be sure your temple will always have a congregation to witness to throughout your day.

Furthermore, every church or temple has different offices that make up the organization, but these offices are not always open. However, as an organism—alive and Spirit-filled—you don't close after office hours. No way! Did Jesus only perform His spiritual duties and ministry in the synagogues or at the temple? No, He did not. He took His office with Him to the streets, the towns, and even the wilderness.

We must understand that Jesus' last name is not Christ. Christ is His official title, also known as Messiah or Anointed

One. He embodied His office wherever He went, becoming the first walking and talking church—body and Head.

> **INSPIRATION:**
> *Preach the word! Be ready in season and out of season. Convince, rebuke, exhort, with all longsuffering and teaching.*
> II TIMOTHY 4:2

And once Jesus—the Head of the church—ascended back into heaven, He left us His Spirit to indwell our temple, the body. Each individual body forms the corporate body—the church body. But a church can't be a living body without being controlled by the Head. Therefore, as a temple, you must take Christ with you wherever you go, knowing that He desires to perform His officiating duties through you. Remember, these "office hours" are 24/7 and 365 days a year. You cannot handle those duties alone, but by His Spirit Who makes you alive.

You may be the only Bible somebody reads, and you may be the only church somebody attends. Without being orderly like a worship service; without offering yourself as a living sacrifice to serve; and without officiating through Christ as His servant, nonbelievers will want nothing to do with your ministry. When will other sinners, sinners just like us, want to invite Christ into their temples for cleansing from the inside out? When we realize that it's important to be a temple who glorifies God in body and spirit. The world says, "If you build it, they will come." But the Word says, "When you let God build *you*, they will come."

Be legible. Be a temple.
Be orderly. Be offering. Be officiating.
Be the Bible!

CHARACTER STAMP:

I MAY B a temple. A temple is a place of praise, prayer, and power. Praise ascends, prayer is offered, and power is expressed. People gather at the temple to fellowship with one another and to worship God. A main purpose of the temple is to invite the presence of God, that His Spirit may fill the people of God. Therefore, as His temple, your body is the place where the Holy Spirit dwells. Are you exhibiting the presence of God? Are you expressing the worship of God? When others come to you, do they find fellowship and sanctuary?
I MAY B a temple.

Preach the Gospel at all times, and when necessary use words.
(attributed to Francis of Assisi)

BOX

-illustration of the law-

To fulfill the law of HIS VESSEL, be a box. Be *better, not battered.*

No! Not a box-cutter. Nothing to do with a box-car. Not even a boxer, and certainly not a box-head. Just a plain old box. A cardboard receptacle that holds its contents for sale, storage, safety or for saving space. We also use boxes for transporting items or stocking items. The box becomes a type of vessel when it is used to hold and carry something other than itself. The humble box!

Here is how we are to be like a box—a concept that holds so much truth. Of course, carrying around the excellence of the power of God, which is Christ, is the main part of it. But when a box, it is about being better by knowing better and doing better. And by striving for better, you won't be battered. And when kept from becoming battered, you will not be bitter.

This is the palpable tactic that will make your "text" legible and even angelic. Take it from me first and then repeat it to yourself often: "Stay in your box!"

> INSPIRATION:
> *But avoid foolish and ignorant disputes, knowing that they generate strife.*
> II TIMOTHY 2:23

When you picture the idea here, imagine a brand-new box with its fresh smell, clean sturdiness, and sharp angles. Fast-forward and picture that same box after it has been used and abused. It is now beaten and battered. Worn down and torn down. Its thick walls are now thin and crushed. It went from useful material to waste material. The box looks weary and exhausted. A botched box!

"Stay in your box!"

"Staying in your box" is SOUL advice for you and your emotions: If you remain poised and in control of yourself, you automatically affect those around you for the good. The more you come out of Christ's character and lose control, the more your "box" is battered. When this becomes a regular occurrence, you begin to take on the personification of a beat-up box—and that is the box you don't want to resemble.

Being like a box is knowing that the object housed within you is the valuable that brings you value. When a store is selling a computer, the lofty price tag is for the computer housed inside the box—not for the lowly box it comes in. Likewise, when

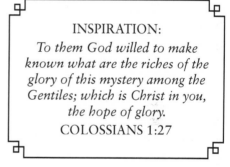

INSPIRATION:
To them God willed to make known what are the riches of the glory of this mystery among the Gentiles; which is Christ in you, the hope of glory.
COLOSSIANS 1:27

the "product" inside of you has value, you hold value. The product, which is Christ in you, is the hope of glory—and that which gives you hope and gives God glory.

You can be a plain old box because Jesus is the one living inside of you and bringing you beauty. He will guard your temperament and keep your composure as your confidence. A balanced box!

When you know that "staying in the box" will keep you from being battered, you can be certain that the Christ in you will make you better. Being read as a box is simply and purely holding and carrying His glory. And rather than boxing you in, it sets you free.

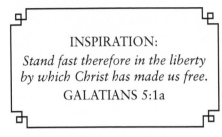

INSPIRATION:
Stand fast therefore in the liberty by which Christ has made us free.
GALATIANS 5:1a

People will try to misuse you, desiring to put their junk inside of you, but you control whether or not your seal is broken. The more you allow your "flaps" to be tampered with, the more damage you begin to take on in your appearance. And by the condition of your "box," those who see you will know that your contents are either treasured or trashed. Hopefully, you are a treasure box!

INSPIRATION:
You will keep Him in perfect peace, whose mind is stayed on You, because he trusts in You.
ISAIAH 26:3

"Stay in your box!" Knowing it is your self-control that makes your box's label legible is half the battle. Then, when people get close enough to read you, you can guarantee that the product on the inside will speak for Himself. Staying in your box is staying in Him!

Be legible. Be a box.
Be better, not battered.
Be the Bible!

CHARACTER STAMP:

I MAY B a box. A box holds, carries, and often stores items. But a box can be damaged by overuse (wear and tear) and misuse (the wrong contents). Thus, being this box is holding, carrying, and storing the character of Christ. Holding boldly, carrying openly, and storing humbly. When we come out of Christ's character, we are doing so at our box's expense. The frame will wear out; the structure will give out. Remaining aware of your fragility keeps intact His integrity.
I MAY B a box.

Carefully calculated steps neutralize calamity.

SHIP

-illustration of the law-

To fulfill the law of HIS VESSEL, be a ship. Be *unsinkable in life by being titanic in Christ.*

They said it was the ship that God Himself could not sink, but this supercilious pride did not prevent the tragic—and ironic—outcome. The *RMS Titanic*, the luxurious British ocean liner that sank in 1912, went down with over a thousand passengers and crew members still on board. The sinking was a result of human error—failure to heed the warnings of "icebergs ahead." That's always how we fall!

A century has passed since the fatal disaster of the *Titanic*, and debates still rage over who was to blame and why. However, arrogance was no doubt a contributing factor, and it is much easier to know what the Word says about pride: *"God resists the proud, but gives grace to the humble"* (I Peter 5:5b).

Grace is given to the humble—the "ship" who is committed to carrying others to their destination, keeping those attached to you from sinking below the waters. As this "ship," you will gracefully glide through life because God's Word has given you Christ. The Greek word for grace, *charis*, means "divine favor or goodwill; that which gives joy; that which is a free gift." This Greek word is also closely related to the word we know in English as "charisma." Do you have *charisma* in Christ?

As a "ship," do you move gracefully like the way of a vessel that moves across the sea? Can those around you have security because of the Captain of your life? Is your outward peace compelling because of your inward propelling, like a ship whose

> INSPIRATION:
> *This charge I commit to you [. . .] having faith and a good conscience, which some having rejected, concerning the faith have suffered shipwreck.*
> I TIMOTHY 1:18-19

rudders operate below the surface but which is the very power that keeps the vessel above the surface?

Being a "ship" is being one who is unsinkable in life because you are a titanic in Christ. You can be certain that storms will brew against you and tidal waves will smash your hull, but even through the squall you're still a legible Bible as HIS VESSEL. It is God's peace and grace that enables you to navigate the storms of life; for when Jesus is being carried on board, nothing will go overboard. His presence grants passage. His commandments demand stillness.

Those in port will closely watch your departure and even anticipate your arrival— some with hate and some with love—but at the end of the journey, all that matters is whether you stayed afloat. Did you get your "passengers" to shore? How did you handle the "tempest tempta-

> INSPIRATION:
> *He calms the storm, so that its waves are still. Then they are glad because they are quiet; so He guides them to their desired haven.*
> PSALM 107:29-30

tions" along the ocean way; did you use the Word to keep the devil at bay?

You can already be certain that your ship is in the binoculars of anchored gazes. Steady eyes awaiting your demise. So with

INSPIRATION:

Now when [Jesus] got into a boat, His disciples followed Him. And suddenly a great tempest arose on the sea, so that the boat was covered with the waves. But He was asleep. Then His disciples came to Him and awoke Him saying, "Lord, save us! We are perishing!" But He said to them, "Why are you fearful, O you of little faith?" Then He arose and rebuked the winds and the sea, and there was a great calm. So the men marveled, saying, "Who can this be, that even the winds and the sea obey Him?"

MATTHEW 8:23-27

these coordinates known, the goal should be to make your faith known. Stay above the water that has drowned others. Suffer successfully by being buoyed in the Bible! According to your ship's manifest, Jesus is with you—a relation*ship* that makes every wave bearable and every water sailable.

Without acknowledging the Captain of your vessel and giving Him the "wheelhouse," your "ship" will be like a rowboat in the sand. Paddling in your own strength and going nowhere. U **MAY B THE ONLY BIBLE SOMEBODY READS,** and that is why you must pay attention to the iceberg heeds and follow where your Captain leads. He knows the waters—in fact, He commands them and walks atop them.

Be legible. Be a ship.
Be unsinkable in life by being titanic in Christ.
Be the Bible!

CHARACTER STAMP:

I MAY B a ship. A ship is a sea-going vessel that transports cargo and people from one port to another. It essentially "floats above" that which can easily drown man. Like a ship, Jesus moved on the water's surface, floating above the danger; when in a relationSHIP with Him, we can do the same. You and those attached to you (on board your ship) have the capability of floating above that which sinks and drowns others. Not because hope floats, but because hope anchors you to the One that does.
I MAY B a ship.

Your voyage is only as unsinkable as your faith.

ILLEGIBLE

-violation of the law-

"But in a great house there are not only vessels of gold and silver, but also of wood and clay, some for honor and some for dishonor" (II Timothy 2:20).

I may have begun with a time when I was legible as HIS VESSEL, but there were plenty of times when I was illegible. It wasn't that I was just unreadable; in fact, I was nonreturnable. Clearly one way! Thus, it is fitting that I share such examples with you that you may learn from my selfish filling and one-way spilling, and do better. It was as if God sent me out time and time again as HIS VESSEL filled with grace, but I never returned the glory. No return on His investment.

I think about how many times God wanted to show me off as His clay pottery, only for me to show myself off, which was selling myself short. No return. I recall how many ministry opportunities God sent my way as His temple, only to close my doors from service, while choosing a vice to serve instead. No return. I recognize how often I came out of my box, battering my own poise, which to God was nothing but noise. No return. And finally, I see how He made me His ship, sent out to help others find land, only to not come back because I had my own plan. No return.

> INFLUENCE:
> *To yield and give way to our passions is the lowest slavery, even as to rule over them is the only liberty.*
> JUSTIN, 100-165 AD

Now, however, I know very well that to fulfill the law HIS VESSEL, there must always be a return. Reciprocity. When God gives, we must take by giving it back to Him. When God fills, we must spill out to glorify Him. When God sends, we must go by staying in His presence. It's a give/get/go thing. God *gives* so much to us in blessings—spiritually, emotionally, financially, mentally, physically—and we *get* to bless others by *going* where He needs us. And then we *get* to *go* and *give* the glory, honor and praise right back to Him. Return.

Sadly, I had misapplied the give/get/go of God's economy, as I would *give* myself credit for *getting* wherever I needed to *go*. I missed the fact that it was God. It was always God who gave and paved. It was always He who would bless, and it was always He who would clean up my mess.

I think back to right before my first year as a professional soccer player, in 2007. In the winter of my senior year at Temple University, I was invited to participate in a professional soccer combine in Tampa, Florida. It was because of my performance there that I found myself chosen as a first-round draft pick in the United Soccer Leagues (USL) College Player Draft. I was selected as the ninth pick overall to the Miami FC, and began my negotiations with that organization immediately.

However, my priority was to graduate and obtain my business degree before commencing my playing career so I had to forfeit my option to Miami, becoming a free agent. During the next few months, while still a student, I was in contact with other pro teams, including the coaches from the Portland Timbers and the Carolina Railhawks. A third pro team, the most unassuming of them all, was a Second Division team in the United Soccer Leagues (USL), while all the other teams were First Division clubs.

This third team seemed to have the most interest in me and would have been a better fit for me. They were the Charlotte

Eagles. The Charlotte Eagles are one of the well-known Christian pro teams in the soccer world. Actually, they may be the only team who identify their entire organization—from front-office staff to owners—as Christians. They take their entire team on mission trips all across the world, where the pro soccer "label" is nothing but a vessel to witness for Jesus Christ and give God the glory.

The coach and organization knew of my faith and soccer ability, making me a very likely candidate to excel within their ranks. Essentially, I was being "called by God" to play pro soccer in the city of Charlotte, which would have been the spiritual view God knew I needed. But I did not answer because I was only interested in the worldly view and what I thought I needed. In retrospect, I even see how strongly this pull was within my spirit, but the flesh of me clearly won that battle.

> INFLUENCE:
> *The beginning of all evil temptations is an unstable mind and a small trust in God. Just as a ship without a helm is tossed about by the waves, so a person who lacks resolution and certainty is tossed about by temptations. Temptation reveals our instability and our lack of trust in God; temptations reveal who we are. This is why we must pay attention to them.*
> THOMAS á KEMPIS, 1380-1471

I cancelled out Charlotte because they were a Second Division team. In spite of the ministry opportunity it presented, I took God's calling as HIS VESSEL and went on my way. I turned down the Charlotte Eagles and decided instead to head down to North Carolina to stay with and train with my older brother's pro team, the Railhawks. Though this placed me in close proximity to the Charlotte Eagles in North Carolina, I was still so far away. I had my flesh made up, which convinced my mind this was the right move.

Eventually I signed a two-year contract with Carolina, which did not pan out for the full two years. I played one season with them before having hernia surgery and that finished the season's performance. My playing rights were then transferred to the New Jersey Ironmen of the Major Indoor Soccer League (MISL), beginning my second year as a pro.

Again, as I look back, I see clearly how I rebelliously missed even the ministry opportunities on both teams. Sure, I was an "Athlete in Action" member and even had my own player card with my testimony on the back, but I was still going through the motions spiritually. The calling was to Charlotte, and I knew it at every soccer step of the way.

Since my rights were now with the New Jersey Ironmen, I did not go back to North Carolina for my second season with the Railhawks. Not because they didn't want me to come back, but because of another hernia surgery at the end of my second year as a pro and my first year with New Jersey, Carolina did not want a liability. In limbo at this point, guess who called me once again? Yep! The Charlotte Eagles. This time, however, I decided to turn them down and go to Miami, the pro team that originally drafted me. I finally answered that call, but quickly found out it was a dropped call. Things did not work out in Miami for several reasons; and instead of stopping to ask God for direction, I continued to plan my own way.

I left Miami and returned to my hometown for the summer of 2008, where I was able to help my older brothers run our First Annual Maher Brothers Soccer Camp. My name would have been on the camp regardless of my presence, and Anthony and Michael were going to run the camp without me even if I were in the middle of a season. But there was no season for me at the time, so I took it as a season of rest. In fact, these camps were a way to give back to the community that had nurtured us as children, and to incorporate our faith and "Character Building Blocks" for the youth.

The camps were a success, but my season of resting was actually a season of festivities. I went out and about more than I had in my entire life. And instead of being HIS VESSEL going where He desired me, I went where I desired me. I may have been seen in the community as a "celebrity," but there is no way God was pleased with me. I was celebrating myself, and an illegible Bible believer at best. I wonder how many people saw me living contrary to my conviction and faith? I wonder—yet, I wonder for nothing because in March of 2009, my example would be on display in *USA TODAY* for everyone to read about.

PRO SOCCER PLAYER INVOLVED IN DRUNK DRIVING FATALITY

The newspapers had put out the appropriate text in one day that my actions had been doing for a while at this point. As within, so without. During that particular season, I violently violated the law of HIS VESSEL. I was given so much and never gave it back to God. I was called to use my gift to glorify God, but I took my gift and glorified myself. I was sent, but I never returned. God was pouring into me to use me, but I was pouring out for me and using God.

> INFLUENCE:
> *If what you are currently doing does not give God glory, then why would He bless it? Not sure about God's will for your life? Practical Insight: Study the life of God's Son and you will discover God's will for every situation.*
> MATTHEW MAHER, 1984-

"There is a way that seems right to a man, but its end is the way of death" (Proverbs 14:12).

VISION RESTORED

Keeping your eyes fixed on the One who formed you is keeping your "I" conformed to the only One who can fix you. God fashioned you as His vessel of honor to use you for His honor. The moment we lose sight of this foresight, our vision becomes blurred and our vessel becomes marred. "For whom He foreknew, He also predestined to be conformed to the image of His Son [...]" (Romans 8:29). *When your sight lines up with this insight, you become a vessel well pleasing in His sight.*
U MAY B HIS VESSEL!

Adopt God's perception as your reality.

PART IX

---

the law of HIS WORKMANSHIP

"God's authorship determines your canvas of influence."

appropriating the law:

*Biblical influence is spherical. Translating this law
is authoring influence. Why? Because the word
"workmanship" in Greek is* poiéma, *and literally means
"a thing made." Are you a thing made, a handiwork, a
masterpiece? Yes! For God makes no mistakes, and you
must be graciously receptive of this.* Poiéma *comes to the
English language as "poem"; so when you know the Great
Author, your "I" finds its canvas of influence by seeing your
life as His masterful workmanship. Again, when your "I"
begins to give Him all the glory, watch how He begins to
write grace to the world around you through your story.*
U MAY B HIS WORKMANSHIP!

Success on earth is a byproduct of living for heaven.

~seeing the law is being the law~

LEGIBLE

-application of the law-

"For we are His workmanship, created in Christ Jesus for good works, which God prepared beforehand that we should walk in them" (Ephesians 2:10).

When projecting the law of HIS WORKMANSHIP, we are to be a legible representation of the *character*, *conduct*, and *conversation* of Jesus Christ.

I like to say that God would not have put His name on us, unless He had already placed the best within us. Knowing we were made in His image ought to obliterate any misconception about how much Almighty God loves us. We are created in His image and similitude. He loves us. He sent His only begotten Son to save us. He loves us.

Notice the root word of "obliterate" is litera, which means "letters," and also forms the words "literate" (able to read and write) and "literacy" (the state of being educated). "Ob" means "against"—thus, "obliterate" means to efface or utterly remove. Hence, because I know (because I am educated, knowledgeable, and biblically literate) that I was created in God's image and character, I therefore know that according to the law of HIS WORKMANSHIP I am a literal masterpiece (an exact translation or precise representation). In fact, the word "workmanship" in Greek is *poiéma*, which means "a thing made," and it comes into English as "poem." The word indicates that we are God's handiwork, masterpiece, and poem. We are His song, His epistle, and even His speech to the world. Essentially, God's authorship determines our canvas of influence.

King David's canvas of influence said it like this, *"For you formed my inward parts; You covered me in my mother's womb. I will praise You, for I am fearfully and wonderfully made; marvelous are Your works, and that my soul knows very well. My frame was not hidden from You, when I was made in secret, and skillfully wrought in the lowest parts of the earth. Your eyes saw my substance being yet unformed. And in Your book they all were written, the days fashioned for me, when as yet there were none of them"* (Psalm 139:13-16).

Wait! Surely to be legible as HIS WORKMANSHIP, we must be wonderful before we can be used by God—or we must work our way into His love, right? Wrong! As David knew, we are wonderfully made because of God's marvelous work. We are the canvas to His authorship. It is Creator God's intention to show us off as His masterpiece to the world and to guard us with His master peace while in the world. Therefore, translating the law of HIS WORKMANSHIP is not writing our own story, but it is allowing God's authorship to determine our canvas of influence for His glory. Surrendering to His key strokes as He types out His literature in our lives for all to read—*"created in Christ Jesus for good works, which God prepared beforehand that we should walk in them."* That's the law of HIS WORK-MANSHIP at work!

When I arrived in prison January 2010, I took the advice of my mom and a good friend that I should keep a journal. Day by day I wrote out my thoughts and feelings as I experienced a world I would never have imagined. After the first week, my mother thought it would be helpful to post some of my entries on Facebook and allow my family and close friends to follow my journey. Despite the jarring encounters and sense of total displacement consistent with life in an alien place, my words were soaked in peace and grace.

My family then decided to create a separate Web site, <www.themattmaherstory.com>, devoted to sharing the story. "I'm That Guy" (see Part III, the law of HIS INSTRUMENT) was paralleled on the Web site and accompanied by a daily blog filled with inspirational anecdotes of hope and faith as I comprehended my situation for God's glory. Within the first few months, there were over 80,000 visitors from all across the globe.

> INFLUENCE:
> *God will make much of Himself through you. But your purpose of heart must be to allow Him to make much of Himself in spite of you. Every factor in your life does not need to be pristine in order for God to work. In truth, "prison" conditions are often the prerequisites to experiencing the Master's peace. Practical Insight: Don't worry about how your situation may look ashy initially . If you give it to God, He'll make it into beauty eventually.*
> MATTHEW MAHER, 1984-

As time went on, the following grew; and it was apparent that from my setting of incarceration, the writings were ministering to people in every demographic. The feedback was collectively encouraging in nature and came from individuals in all walks of life. People were reading a legible result from tragedy to the daily work toward triumph. Peace from prison. The viewers shared how their own outlook on life was altered drastically because of my story.

With all humility, the blog translated the law of HIS WORKMANSHIP to show the reader His grace in my life. Without Him, I couldn't; and without me, He wouldn't—meaning, being the only Bible somebody may read motivated me to write the blog with biblical perspectives in a consistent and clear manner. The story would not be a story at all had it not given God glory. So, without Him, I can't. And the story could not have been blessed by God had I not shared it. So, without me, He won't.

It would have been easier to close myself off from the world and do my time in silent anonymity, but I learned early on that

> INFLUENCE:
> *It must be understood that our wickednesses are entirely our own, but our goodnesses pertain both to the Almighty God and to ourselves.*
> GREGORY the GREAT, 540-604 AD

it wasn't about me. Sure I was the antagonist to my fate and responsible for recklessly causing an innocent man's death by my choice to drink and drive, but God declares in His Word that He works all things together for good. Therefore, I had to give Him my circumstances in order for me to become His canvas of influence. I had to forfeit my own inclinations and allow God to turn "my" story into a masterpiece for His glory. I had to faithfully write out the blog entries that He placed on my heart to share. And I learned to see Him in all that each day held, even submerged in the evil and chaos of prison.

Consequently, though I am hardly a master of my native tongue, English, the story has been translated into 67 different languages. The blog has been read by over a half-million people (and counting) in every state and in 121 different countries. All because I recognized that in spite of my tragic behavior, God loves me, forgives me, and wants to use me as His "blog" to the world. Again, without Him and His amazing grace, I can't. With God and His grace, I can.

The blog has been the "Bible" that visitors are able to read. Legible. As God's masterpiece and handiwork, it's important to take our hands off our circumstances in order to let God go to work with our circumstances (BLOGS, Volumes I-IV, at 55:11 Publishing).

POEM

-illustration of the law-

To translate the law of HIS WORKMANSHIP, be a poem. Be *composed*, *creative*, and *cadenced*.

God, a poet? You better believe it! He thought you out before He wrote you out. He did not neglect a single detail in your life, making each and every word connect with rhythmic flow into the next line. Every event and each experience has purpose in this composition called life, where a relationship with the poem's Composer ought to bring a peaceable composure. How so? Because you know that at the end of each line is a rhyme; so whatever happens next in life must transitionally work out just fine.

> INSPIRATION:
> *And we know that all things work together for good to those who love God, to those who are the called according to His purpose.*
> ROMANS 8:28

Even when you can't see the purpose in your circumstance, since you are a poem, you can boldly take your faith stance. Composed under adverse pressure because God knows how to verse measure. He will never allow you to be tempted beyond what you are able, so when read like a

> INSPIRATION:
> *He has shown you, O man, what is good; and what does the Lord require of you but to do justly, to love mercy, and to walk humbly with your God?*
> MICAH 6:8

poem by others you will remain legibly stable. People watch to see if your flesh or eyes will lust, but let them see you die to yourself by remaining poetically just. You are a poem because you know Him!

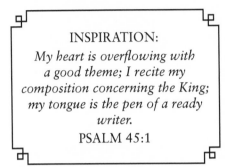

INSPIRATION:

My heart is overflowing with a good theme; I recite my composition concerning the King; my tongue is the pen of a ready writer.

PSALM 45:1

Be the poem that others can joyfully recite, not doggerel of gloom or spite. It's your talents that point back to the Poet; and when people ask how you did this or that, you'll let them know it: "It was for God's glory, for He gave me this ability to be innovative. And without Him, there's no way I can be this creative!"

Be a poem, lyrically cadenced and flowing. Step by step and line by line, God's glory is showing. No matter what you say or do, what is being expressed? Are you being read as upbeat or down and depressed? God's poetry is always under control with good themes, so as His poem, do others know what your faith even means? You walk by faith and not by sight. So when it's dark, you are still light.

INSPIRATION:

Looking unto Jesus, the author and finisher of our faith.

HEBREWS 12:2a

U MAY BE THE ONLY BIBLE SOMEBODY READS! Therefore, be the only poem that somebody needs. You make others feel good for your conversation that's pleasant. Even without using words, they know good conduct is present. Being a poem is not about external eloquence and line flow, but having an inner character that lets Jesus' rhymes show. You are HIS WORKMANSHIP, a poem pricelessly priced. But here is the ultimate question—do others know your Author is Christ?

Be legible. Be a poem.
Be composed. Be creative. Be cadenced.
Be the Bible!

CHARACTER STAMP:

I MAY B a poem. A poem is a composition in verse that often rhymes with creative flow. It's also metrical writing that is systematic in form and precise in structure. Removing one line or even one word can set the entire stanza off-balance. Each phrase needs the next to form the line that makes rhythmic sense. Thus, your life is a poem, when your life poetically shows Him. Each word and work is balanced by the whole; be read as His workmanship, the sum of your goal.
I MAY B a poem.

Your eloquent talk carries only as much weight as the balance of your walk.

SONG

-illustration of the law-

To translate the law of HIS WORKMANSHIP, be a song. Be *rapping, while rocking and rolling.*

Sing a song! Become a song and sing along with God's symphony. Sometimes rapping it out. Sometimes rocking it out. But always rolling it out in order to extol it out. When you first decide to get in tune with God's music, it is done by "voice checking," which is "care casting." The Apostle Peter writes, *"casting all your care upon Him, for He cares for you" (I Peter 5:7).* The word "cast" can mean "to roll"—as in "roll the die." So when we cast, we are actually "rolling our cares upon the Lord"—the Rock—that we may sing loud and clear without having a strained tone. Rocking and rolling! Cacophony is replaced with harmony!

It is not always the best voice that makes a good song because sometimes a song is made by its lyrics. The actions that your life raps will have others considering the music. They may not understand the movements at first, but your melodic backbeat will reveal a consistent flow of faith. You see, life may have been trying to beat you back, but based on your "rocking and rolling" technique, you are able to rap your way through with

> INSPIRATION:
> *The Lord is my strength and song, and He has become my salvation; He is my God, and I will praise Him; my father's God, and I will exalt Him.*
> EXODUS 15:2

a backbeat that's true. It's not lyrical perfection that makes you legible, rather it's your lyrics' direction that makes you readable. Forward by faith. Are you rapping about yourself with strong words? Or is the Lord your strength and song as you live by His word?

Because the Lord sings a strong song, to be the only Bible somebody may read simply requires us to just sing along. Since His words are already established, when you couple your voice with His, you become part of His opus and He enables you to do it. Do what? Live as a song that leads others to the faith. And not because of your own melody, but purely by God's saving grace!

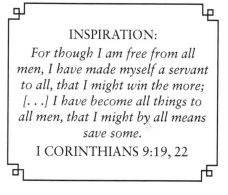

INSPIRATION:
For though I am free from all men, I have made myself a servant to all, that I might win the more; [. . .] I have become all things to all men, that I might by all means save some.
I CORINTHIANS 9:19, 22

Be ready to embody every genre of music that you may offer a song to others in their time of need. In need of comfort: You can sing softly in their pain. In need of motivation: You can sing upbeat, and let them follow your lead. In need of peace: You can sing to them Christ, which is praying in Jesus' name over their life. All genres to all men!

Is your life's song in perfect pitch? Integrity filled. Or is it a voiceover that tries to get over? Deceit willed.

No one is impressed by a lip-syncher, nor is anyone influenced by lip service. Those listening to your song will want to see your voice line up with your choice. Your talk backed up by your walk. Dancing out what you're singing about. Being a strong song is living life so others nod their heads and win, rather than shaking their heads as you sin. Does your song sing Bible or babel?

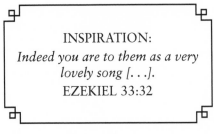

INSPIRATION:
Indeed you are to them as a very lovely song [. . .].
EZEKIEL 33:32

When you know God is producing the music in your life, you can be certain that He will use you and your circumstances as HIS WORKMANSHIP to save souls. Like a choral progression that soothes the listener's soul, so your life will be to others when you learn to rock and roll!

Be legible. Be a song.
Be rapping. Be rocking and rolling.
Be the Bible!

CHARACTER STAMP:

I MAY B a song. A song is vocal music. Whether rung out, rapped out or bellowed out, a song is a composition of words set to a musical tune. A song can uniquely affect your mood. As a song affects the emotions, so must you be the song that reflects Jesus' vibrations. His melody is already set, and by musically tuning into His Word you will be on the right track. Not just instrumental imitation, but harmonious impartation.
I MAY B a song.

Let your life's song be conducted by the Savior.

EPISTLE

-illustration of the law-

To translate the law of HIS WORKMANSHIP, be an epistle. Be *signed*, *sealed*, and *sent*.

No, an epistle is not an apostle's wife! An epistle is a letter with instruction and inspiration. In fact, the books that Paul contributed to the Bible are classified as epistles. Instructional, directional, and correctional in nature. They were also signed for credibility, sealed for security, and sent for delivery. Thus, when we become an epistle of Christ, we too are signed by the Father, sealed by the Holy Spirit, and sent by the Son. We can pray, "Signed, sealed, delivered, I'm Yours!" knowing that God will lead us where He needs us.

As an epistle, you provide more than just information to your reader. As a matter of fact and as a matter of tact, you provide revelation to your reader. You present grace and truth. Grace to appeal and truth to reveal. Your content brings substance that sustains, through teaching and preaching. Your wisdom's value is often documented in experience. Those reading you as an epistle can tell the difference whether your information is plagiarized or authorized. Is it pretentious advice or righteous advisement?

By being authentic in your approach as an epistle you can rest assured that because God signed you, sealed you, and sent you, He will enable you by going with you. No matter what you are going through or where you are in life, you will be enveloped by His peace.

> INSPIRATION:
> *Now He who establishes us with you in Christ and has anointed us is God, who also has sealed us and given us the Spirit in our hearts as a guarantee.*
> II CORINTHIANS 1:21-22

Furthermore, your words and actions have syntax, grammatically structured to make sense. It's not rambling in what you represent or gambling on whether you will be received. Rather, it is having the confidence that as an epistle of Christ, you will be written out by the Spirit of the living God. Signed with the blood. Sealed by the blood. And sent for the blood. Therefore, you must believe that your postage can handle any tribulation you go through—you are stamped by the blood, because you were bought by the blood.

Having your inspiration rejected and not received should not discourage you because once you've committed to being mailed out there is no telling where you will end up. Perhaps you will be sent before your haters or enemies, yet their read of you ought to be clear. They may not heed you after they read you, but at least they know that what was expressed was in honor of the Name on your return address. Signed by THE WAY, sealed by THE TRUTH, and sent by THE LIFE. Jesus the Christ.

> INSPIRATION:
> *You are our epistle written in our hearts, known and read by all men; clearly you are an epistle of Christ, ministered by us, written not with ink but by the Spirit of the living God, not on tablets of stone but on tablets of flesh, that is, of the heart.*
> II CORINTHIANS 3:2-3

Epistles are made to be opened. No one can know what your parchment says until you become transparent and readable. Not ashamed of your blemished past or smudged mistakes. Such errors have been erased by

Christ on the cross. Therefore, they must be embraced by you in order to relate to others with the purpose of being able to legibly point them to Christ.

> INSPIRATION:
> *Let such a person consider this, that what we are in word by letters when we are absent, such we will also be in deed when we are present.*
> II CORINTHIANS 10:11

Paul's epistles were effective when he was absent, but only because they were backed by his actions when he was present. So, too, will nobody care what you know until they know that you care. You are God's letter to the world. This doesn't make you better than the world, but it certainly makes you live better by the Word.

Be legible. Be an epistle.
Be signed. Be sealed. Be sent.
Be the Bible!

CHARACTER STAMP:

I MAY B an epistle. "Epistle" is another word for "letter," and it can specifically refer to the New Testament letters written by the apostles. The apostles' epistles were intended to instruct the church on behavior, belief, and doctrine centered in Christ. If writing on ancient parchment could accomplish so much, how much greater could be your influence? You can, and you will—when you purpose in your heart to bring the ink from God's letters to life.
I MAY B an epistle.

Transfigure ink into instinct.

SPEECH

-illustration of the law-

To translate the law of HIS WORKMANSHIP, be a speech. Be *the eternal echo of the temporary tomb.*

The Word became flesh and stepped to the podium of the Cross. With no microphone or other assisted audio devices, He gave His last speech that still reverberates throughout all dimensions of time and space and realms today. With eternal eloquence, it took three days for the sound of this speech to echo from earth to heaven and back again.

You see, the Word knew something that many still don't understand. He knew that His own pain would be our comfort. The world was forever changed by God's speech expressed in Jesus Christ, the Word, leaving us with the blessed opportunity to "be the eternal echo of the temporary tomb."

Christ was His final spoken word to mankind; now we are this powerful speech's recitation—still being watched and heard with scrutiny from the audience of the world. Is your life applaudable? Is it even audible? Legible?

It is often the pitch that gives away the feelings we have toward the subject of our spoken speech. But when you're the personification of a speech, sometimes you have to forfeit your own feelings in order to honor the audience you're trying to reach. Your speech should stress faith, not feelings, like body language that helps drive home a point. Just as voice modulation and carefully timed pauses are the speaker's tools to persuade, so must you effectively live in order to engage your listeners.

> INSPIRATION:
>
> *God, who at various times and in various ways spoke in time past to the fathers by the prophets, has in these last days spoken to us by His Son [. . .] who being the brightness of His glory and the express image of His person, and upholding all things by the word of His power [. . .].*
> HEBREWS 1:1-3

Sadly, slandering of the Word occurs when we choose to change the speech's theme. As His speech, the only way God's character can be heard by the world is if you live by the Word. The moment your conduct does not line up with the Word, your speech becomes a breach. That is why it is not what you know, but what you show.

Being a speech is living out the spoken Word of God—not just by imitation of Christ, but by impartation of Christ. Here's the mega-difference: Imitating is just doing Christ-like things, which is like training a monkey to sing like a human, but you are still controlled by self as the monkey is still a monkey. Impartation, however, is when you allow His speech to reside in you—that isn't Christ-like, it's Christ's life! Alive in Christ! Essentially, it's bringing the Bible to life.

Being His speech is allowing the heart of the Word to be felt through you. Many in the audience of life do not understand God or they may have misinterpreted something they heard about Him. They may base their conclusions on confusion, such as, "Why would a loving God allow that?" Because they won't read Him for themselves to discover the truth, you can be sure they will read you. Will they see the Truth?

> **INSPIRATION:**
> *Let my teaching drop as rain, my speech distill as the dew, as raindrops on the tender herb, and as showers on the grass.*
> DEUTERONOMY 32:2

Your life should make His discourse clear by staying the course that He gave us to adhere. How do you do this? By knowing that God spoke it; now all you have to do is make His presentation your dedication so that others can know it. Remember, a speech is not a speech because of the spoken word. No! A speech is a speech because it is heard!

Be legible. Be a speech.
Be the eternal echo of the temporary tomb.
Be the Bible!

CHARACTER STAMP:

I MAY B speech. A speech is a public talk or lecture intended to convey a message to a listening audience. A speech can be used to explain, proclaim, and even to entertain. Often, the most compelling speeches come from the orator's personal experiences. Likewise, you may be this type of speech, sometimes delivered without saying a word.
I MAY B a speech.

Own the podium by leading, even when not speaking.

ILLEGIBLE

-violation of the law-

"What I speak, I speak not according to the Lord, but as it were, foolishly, in this confidence of boasting" (II Corinthians 11:17).

I may have begun with a time when I was legible as HIS WORKMANSHIP, but there were plenty of times when I was illegible. It wasn't that I was just unreadable; in fact, I was carnal. Clearly worldly! Thus it is fitting that I share such examples with you that you may learn from my resume and know better to do better. I can assure you that because I was visible in the world's eyes and appeared to be doing well, that all was not well. My past life was far from God's masterpiece or poem, and closer to an example that stressed I didn't know Him!

You are the only one who can examine your resume and ask yourself whether it is glorifying God in the Spirit or glorifying self in the flesh. Like Paul, I boast in my past resume, but only to show you that it is now my obituary. I boast foolishly in the worldly things to share with you that it is all rubbish in comparison to life in Christ. Furthermore, I was nothing but a fool to boast even at the time.

Illegible and visible—a very dangerous combination, for it makes up the resume of a fool; and this fool was far from using his resume as

> INFLUENCE:
> *The world is God's, but the worldly is the devil's.*
> TERTULLIAN, 160-230 AD

God's workmanship tool. Since **U MAY B THE ONLY BIBLE SOMEBODY READS**, know that God's word is the only resume that one will ever need. Listen up!

I gotta get real to make sure I give the right appeal. None of this is to be glorified, and with this resume comes nothing fortified. You want this life? Take note that I'm writing this from prison; this resume wasn't life, it was foolishly livin'. All this talk about it being "the life"—the worldly dreams that we pursue. Well, let us talk about it then, 'cause I'll show you where it will lead you!

I'm not talking about having passions and possessions when aligned with the right view. I'm talking about the wrong perspective, when your possessions and passions own you. Wanna talk about what the devil doesn't want you to see? Let's get to it then, as I let my past resume do the talking for me:
Wanna talk alcohol? Dom P's, Moëts—I popped 'em!
Wanna talk clubs? VIP's, open tabs—I hopped 'em!
Wanna talk clothes? Burberry, Purple Label—I shopped 'em!
Wanna talk diamonds? Wrist, neck, ears—I rocked 'em!
Wanna talk cars? Escalades, 750s—I jocked 'em!
Wanna talk fights? Brawls, broken bones to bullies—I knocked'em!
Wanna talk girls? Models, dancers, eyes—I locked 'em!
Wanna talk sports? Division 1, first-round pick to pro—I topped 'em!
Wanna talk casinos? Pent suites, wines and dines—I comped 'em!

What do you wanna talk about today, "the life" that's glorified on the surface resume or the truth behind it all—that has me living behind the wall? It's not a poem, a speech, an epistle, or a song! I clearly violated the law of HIS WORKMANSHIP, with a lifestyle oh-so-wrong.

Listen up! The above is the resume of a fool. Don't get it twisted for one second; none of that is the definition of cool. Cool is staying calm when the overwhelming pressure is on.

Cool is standing up for what's right regardless of the majority strong. Cool is being yourself and not conforming to a mold. Cool is warm with gentleness and love, and has nothing to do with cold. Cool is integrity and the WAY that Christ walked. Cool is accountability and the TRUTH that Christ talked. Cool is the one who mans up for his faith. Cool is the LIFE that knows in Christ he is safe!

> INFLUENCE:
> *If we are not our own, but the Lord's, it is clear to what purpose all our deeds must be directed. We are not our own, therefore neither our reason nor our will should guide us in our thoughts and actions. We are not our own, therefore we should not seek what is only expedient to the flesh. We are not our own, therefore let us forget ourselves and our own interests as far as possible.*
> JOHN CALVIN, 1509-1564

This resume is now my obituary and a document that holds no glory. If you think that it does, I suggest you watch the "I'm That Guy" story. Pathetic I was and blinded by the world's sights; if the flashing begins to hurt, know that you're following the wrong lights—

This was the opposite of the law of HIS WORKMANSHIP, and was actually indicative of my own authorship. During this worldly season of my life, outward looks were deceiving because nothing was internally nice. I'll end by reiterating and agreeing with what Paul came to know: *"But what things were gain to me, these I have counted loss for Christ. Yet indeed I also count all things loss for the excellence of the knowledge of Christ Jesus my Lord, for whom I have suffered the loss of all things, and count them as rubbish, that I may gain Christ and be found in Him, not having my*

> INFLUENCE:
> *Fear not failure. But fear success in things that are godless.*
> *Practical Insight: Write out your spiritual resume—your goals of God, your gifts from God, your giving for God—and compare it with your work history.*
> MATTHEW MAHER, 1984-

own righteousness, which is from the law, but that which is through faith in Christ, the righteousness which is from God by faith" (Philippians 3:7-9).

VISION RESTORED

In order to see yourself most dearly, you must first see Christ most clearly. Your personality was designed perfectly for you and you alone, but the only One who can pull it out of you is the One who placed it inside of you. When you no longer try to mold yourself, and simply let God unfold yourself, you will begin to know yourself as an awesome creation made by the Wonderful Creator. David wrote, "For you formed my inward parts; You covered me in my mother's womb. I will praise You, for I am fearfully and wonderfully made; marvelous are Your works, and that my soul knows very well" (Psalm 139:13-14).
U MAY B HIS WORKMANSHIP!

See His works' wonders to know you're His wonderful work.

PART X

---

the law of HIS BODY

"The extremity of your soul is Christ's mind and manners on earth:
As His, so yours."

appropriating the law:

Biblical influence is flexible. When you reach out to the Head—Christ—you become the outreach of Him. Thus, your "I" will only be as effective as the mind that motivates you. "[W]e have the mind of Christ" (I Corinthians 2:16). When you allow His mind to exercise your body, you will be capable of positively impacting anybody. However, His central nervous system must be your system of service no matter the system in which you serve. Church system; family system; school system; corporate system; government system; military system; prison system; and so on. Your "I" is part of His body and may be the very body that brings somebody to the only One who can save anybody. "I" test your soul by feeling for His.
U MAY B HIS BODY!

Reveal His mind through your manner.

~seeing the law is being the law~

LEGIBLE

-application of the law-

"Now you are the body of Christ, and members individually"
(I Corinthians 12:27).

When projecting the law of HIS BODY, we are to be a legible representation of the *character, conduct,* and *conversation* of Jesus Christ.

I like to think of it like this! Wherever your feet take you, let your body speak for the Word. And when necessary use words! When exercising the law of HIS BODY, the language of the body needs to be an extension of grace; the heart needs to be an invitation of love; the limbs need to be the agents of peace; the scars need to be a reference of healing. Tactically, even our body adornment—clothing, hair styles, jewelry, etc.—should line up with an inward change and transformation.

Ultimately, we are to exercise the law of HIS BODY by the way we are charitable toward everybody, never using or abusing anybody, while knowing you are somebody, and keeping the gospel from nobody. Paul wrote, *"[B]ut with boldness, as always, so now also Christ will be magnified in my body, whether by life or death"* (Philippians 1:20). Paul knew that the body's conduct would be the only way for the world to legibly see the head, Christ. How we conduct our external being ought to make Christ, our internal being, ever more conspicuous.

Wait! Surely to be legible as HIS BODY we must be clean-cut on the outside, with no piercings, scars or tattoos, right?

> ### INFLUENCE:
>
> *Faith is not an accessory; it's access to God's economy. And according to His economy, even the story behind a tattoo presents a gospel opportunity. And not just a tattoo, but also any avenue that accentuates God's grace. Practical Insight: Survival breeds confidence; and since God was faithful back then, He'll be faithful again. Lean into such timeless past graces to birth confidence of faith in the present.*
>
> MATTHEW MAHER, 1984-

Wrong! I'm not suggesting body art as a representation of your faith; but for those of us who have body art, please know that it's possible to use your body as art from the heart! Being HIS BODY has nothing to do with lewdness or nudeness, and everything to do with being an opportunist—taking every opportunity to bring the Bible's ink to life, where the extremity of your soul is Christ's outreach on earth. That's the flexibility in the law of HIS BODY.

In April 2009, just six weeks after the fatal tragedy, my parents allowed me to accompany them on their annual vacation to Florida. It would be an opportunity to get away from the negative spotlight that my actions brought upon my entire family, but also a time to remember God's faithfulness from the past. It was written all over me, but it took several strangers to pull it out of me by reading it on me.

I was in an emotional state of shock at this time, and my body was still recovering from surgery that took place five days after the accident for a soccer injury—repair for a torn ACL(anterior cruciate ligament). Yet here I was in Florida, trying to act like every other vacationer by relaxing, but I was unable to vacate my surreal circumstances, which were emotionally and physically taxing.

I spent part of each day in the resort's hot tub—thinking, praying, and doing knee rehabilitation exercises. I would have preferred to be left in solitude, not bothered by anyone, but God had other plans for my body.

I found myself surrounded by a group of 10 women, who were also on vacation. Ranging in age from 24 to 50, they were enjoying a "ladies' getaway" from their homes in New York. The most personable one of the group, Deb,

> INFLUENCE:
> *No soul will ever grow deep in the spiritual life unless God works passively in that soul by means of the dark night.*
> JOHN of the CROSS, 1542-1591

began the conversation by asking about my tattoos. Within an hour, the women learned almost everything about my past life because of the artwork on my body. They also got a history lesson on my former profession as a soccer player because of the knee injury.

The women learned that I was the youngest of four boys, born into a family of faith. They asked about the Bible verse on my arm, Proverbs 3:5, and its meaning. They wanted to know about my family crest, which appears on my back. They asked about my parents and the little girl they had seen with me earlier in the day. "Whose daughter is that?" they inquired.

They had observed me with my 3-year-old niece, Alivia, which presented the opportunity to explain that her father (my brother) had passed away in December of 2005. Naturally, they wanted to know how a young man had died (John was 28 at the time of his death), so I told them "how" by stressing "Who." "Who" was God, Who sustains us by His grace even in times of tragedy.

On my left rib is the memorial tattoo to this event. With Jesus holding my brother in His heavenly embrace, I am reminded of God's faithfulness to my family and to me. While these women were reading my body, they may not have understood that they were actually giving me the opportunity to represent HIS BODY—particularly to myself, as these remembrances ministered to me.

Eventually, Deb and Tracy came over to meet my parents. They then introduced the rest of their group to my family. For the next several days, they regularly stopped by to talk when we were all gathered at the pool area. Little did we know that they had googled me on the first day we had met, and thereby learned about the tragic accident for which I was facing prison. Yet, that daunting information did not deter them. In fact, it seemed to intrigue them, and they were encouraged to "read" me and my family further. Deb, Tracy, and Barb actually pulled my mom aside to encourage her about my situation, and to let her know how proud she should be in the way I conducted myself around them.

Body art was the avenue by which I was able to speak openly about my faith. Faith that I needed to have pulled out of me by these strangers. Faith that attracted several of them to stay in touch with us in the months and years that followed. Four years later, I am still in contact with Deb, Tracy, and Barb via mail, and they offer steady support to my mom via e-mail.

We would not share this friendship today had I closed off my testimony on the first day we met—sealed my lips and kept to myself, as I had wished. I take no credit for being legible to the women. But I know that by exercising the law of HIS BODY, even our tattoos can prompt conversations about faith. In this case, at this time in my life, I was the Bible that *I* needed to read, and to heed.

> INFLUENCE:
> *It is in many ways a grander virtue and a more splendid achievement to cure the weaknesses of one's own soul than those of the body of another.*
> JOHN CASSIAN, 360-345 AD

It is amazing how God used these women to remind me of all that God had written over my life up to that point. The beautiful art of His grace was already inked on my body. Legible reminders of His love, mercy, forgiveness, peace, almighty power and control.

However, the ink on my body alone is not the art. No! The ink on my body was the jumpstart that caused me to open up the recesses of my heart—interesting anecdotes for them; intimate answers for me.

BODY LANGUAGE

-illustration of the law-

To exercise the law of HIS BODY, be His body language. Be *the embodiment of language.*

Say a lot by not saying anything at all. Some days you may have nothing to say, nothing to say! And that's OK! You may want to speak, but you must train your tongue first. Why? Because the tongue, the most powerful muscle we possess, holds the language that can curse or bless! When you have nothing beneficial to say, the best example is to refrain from giving wordy evidence of that fact.

INSPIRATION:
But [Jesus] answered him not one word, so that the governor marveled greatly.
MATTHEW 27:14

Aside from the tongue, there is another language we embody—the language that we speak with our body. Sometimes this language speaks louder and plainer than our words, and it can be the dialect that makes or breaks our connection to others. The language of the body can be abrasive—screaming "curses" of exasperation, impatience, dislike, and disinterest with movements such as frowning, rolling the eyes, prolonged staring or refusal to make eye contact, excessive sighing or throat clearing, slouching, a weak handshake or no handshake. Such body language is deliberately aggressive and intentionally offensive, and observers are afraid to come close. Contrary to the abrasive body language is the body language that speaks gentleness and peace; by such a disposition, we give an approachable proposition.

Perhaps your mother, like mine, told you that your facial expressions spoke louder than your verbal professions. Sometimes this admonition will catch us off-guard because we cannot see ourselves,

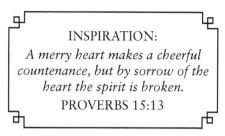

INSPIRATION:
A merry heart makes a cheerful countenance, but by sorrow of the heart the spirit is broken.
PROVERBS 15:13

and therefore we often think our body's language belongs to us alone—unaware are we that others are "reading" us. Hence, being the embodiment of language necessitates controlling your output, knowing that it is being read as the doctrine you put out. It may not be what you said and it may not be your precise actions, but the body language expresses what you actually meant to say or do.

For example, my father would be quick to remind me that my athletic posture, which was poised and confident, could be mistaken for lazy and complacent. He knew that at first glance, a coach is more inclined to notice readiness and hustle over a relaxed and comfortable bearing. Likewise, as His body language, are you able to speak strength without speaking at length? Is your countenance expressing the peace of the Word without your voice expressing a piece of word?

Behavioral and law enforcement specialists study mannerisms because people lie, but body language tells the truth. You must learn to speak and interpret two languages—that of the tongue and that of the body. Both are able to sting curses or sing blessings.

As Charles Spurgeon said in one of his sermons:

The most depraved and despised classes of society formed an inner ring of hearers around our Lord. I gather from this that He was a most approachable person, that He was not of repulsive manners, but that He courted human confidence and was willing that men should commune with Him.

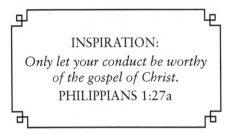

INSPIRATION:
Only let your conduct be worthy of the gospel of Christ.
PHILIPPIANS 1:27a

We want to be as approachable as Jesus. A few steps in developing positive body language reflective of Jesus would be: exercising good hygiene—clean teeth, hair, nails, and clothes; friendly eye contact; good posture; and conversation that focuses on the other person—express interest by remembering names and personal details. Remember, **U MAY B THE ONLY BIBLE SOMEBODY READS!**

In tongue and in body, the goal is to have both your languages read with interest and not with insolence. Try to speak more without saying more.

Be legible. Be His body language.
Be the embodiment of language.
Be the Bible!

CHARACTER STAMP:

I MAY B body language. There is another language we embody, and that is the language that we speak with our bodies. This language can speak louder than words and can also be the language that connects or rejects. Thus, when you are in control of your disposition, you can effectively give an attractive proposition—by controlling your body language. I MAY B body language.

Know that you are speaking the Word even when not saying a word by your body language.

HEART

-illustration of the law-

To exercise the law of HIS BODY, be His heart. Be *core caring*, *core cleaning*, and *core convicting*.

Your heart's a throne! Depending on who is king, your heart becomes either a hole or a home. For this book's intended purposes, we will assume Christ is the One sitting on the throne of your heart, making your heart His heart and your core His home. It is His heart that others must see if they're going to be set free. If we are HIS BODY, then our lives must show off God's heart as we pulsate with purpose. Just as blood is pumped by the heart and circulates throughout the body, so too does Christ's blood flow through His entire body, desiring to circulate through us to touch others. Everybody.

Representing the King's heart is being an ambassador that core cares: beating consistently with faith, and bleeding compassion on others. There are so many hearts out there that are broken and in need of fixing. Heart aches and heart breaks make the nonbeliever vulnerable to the surgeries that the world has to offer. Vices and entices. Such procedures only leave them temporarily numb until inevitable heart failure comes. But their heart conditions are also an opportunity to capitalize on their vulnerability by presenting them heartfelt care. Not medi-care, but core care!

INSPIRATION:
Blessed are the pure in heart, for they shall see God.
MATTHEW 5:8

When you show other hearts that His heart cares, the numbness of the world begins to fade away, which makes a way for core cleaning. Mending. Filling. And ultimately sealing. You can expect to meet opposition—heart attacked—when you get this close to someone else's pain. Like the scalpel that cuts away a tumor, getting one step closer to the operation's success, only to encounter the impediment of a blood clot. So too does the devil step in when he knows that one of his hearts is about to meet Christ's heart. And once the core convicting starts, the devil's efforts fall apart. Expect such attacks from the wicked one by keeping your heart shielded in faith.

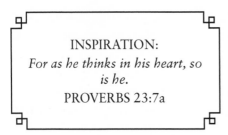

INSPIRATION:
For as he thinks in his heart, so is he.
PROVERBS 23:7a

Knowing that Christ's heart pumps pure blood that covers the world's sins is recognizing that His is the only heart you need to wear on your sleeve to soul win. Wearing your own heart is like wearing sin, but when you take on the personification of His heart then blood transfusions begin.

Shattered hearts have a hard time reading a book of self-help or a brochure on depression. They may complete the suggested reading, but the reading does nothing to complete them. This is why you can be certain that they will be reading you in desperation. But that is exactly the right time when you can offer them your medication by core caring for their pain, core cleaning in Jesus' name, and core convicting by helping them deal with their guilt and shame.

Don't be afraid to tell them about your previous heart condition, which was once beaten by sin and left you with an aching hole in your heart. Your honest testimony will assure them that you can relate to their heartache. But then you tell them how your heart is now filled with love because the King of Kings sits on the throne of your heart. His home. And He is the One Who makes your heart pristine clean, no longer shackled by filth and weighed down by guilt.

His heart will be read clearly in your life when you allow others to get near to your life. Transparency will promote transfusion. The more open you are about your faith, the more interested others will be about this free gift called grace. And remember: As a representative of the King's heart, you are not only covered by the blood, but you are a vessel that carries His blood. You become His heart's steady beat that helps others deal with their painful palpitations. The sorrow of the world leads to death and devastation, but godly sorrow that comprehends the blood leads to hope and salvation. Legible heartburn is concern for others!

> INSPIRATION:
> *But His word was in my heart like a burning fire shut up in my bones;I was weary of holding it back, and I could not.*
> JEREMIAH 20:9b

Be legible. Be His heart.
Be core caring. Be core cleaning. Be core convicting.
Be the Bible!

CHARACTER STAMP:

I MAY B a heart. A heart beats with rhythmic contractions and keeps the circulation of blood flowing through the body. However, since antiquity, the heart is also the organ considered to be the seat of emotions and is synonymous with love. Thus, the heart is vital for life, and can even be the sum of one's whole personality. Therefore, when you start with your heart by asking God to "create in you a clean heart," then the ensuing circulation of blood will be Jesus' from above.
Cleansed to be heartily clear in thought and sight.
I MAY B *a heart.*

Govern your heart, for out of it flows your state.

LIMBS

-illustration of the law-

To exercise the law of HIS BODY, be His limbs. Be *projecting* and *connecting*.

Our own body can teach us much of the functions of HIS BODY. For example, when my foot would score a goal in a soccer match, my whole body would rejoice. Every muscle in my face would break out in a smile. My arms would shoot up in the sky. Then my teammates would feel the goal connection, and their bodies would react like mine—even connecting with mine in the celebration dance. The same effect holds true if I were to stub my toe. The pain travels from the point of impact to the foot. My leg responds by limping to protect the foot from further injury. The rest of my body moves in a way to keep me upright while my balance is compromised. Again, my teammates would react with sympathy and may even rush in to assist me. The body is a whole, and each member is affected by each function. In the gain and in the pain.

It would make no sense for my hand to get mad at my foot for scoring that goal. And it would be illogical for my mouth to break into hearty laughter when my toe has been jammed or sprained. Yet that is the conflict we

> INSPIRATION:
> *For as the body is one and has many members, but all the members of that one body, being many, are one body, so also is Christ. [. . .] And the eye cannot say to the hand, "I have no need of you"; nor again the head to the feet, "I have no need of you."*
> I CORINTHIANS 12:12, 21

represent when we attack other members of the body of Christ. Laughing at another person's mistakes or misfortunes. Bitter toward another person's blessings. Such "bodily functions" are what the nonbelievers prey on, and such disputes ought to be what we as HIS BODY pray on. We need to be attractive by our hARMony, hoping to add to our Christian ARMy!

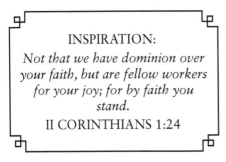

INSPIRATION:

Not that we have dominion over your faith, but are fellow workers for your joy; for by faith you stand.

II CORINTHIANS 1:24

Being His limbs is walking in a manner that projects the gospel of peace wherever your feet take you and in spite of how other people receive you. That's the goal! Walking circumspectly regardless of your circumstances. Sometimes it is not even about where you go, but how you stand. Are your legs established in the faith no matter what you face? How you use your limbs is not dependent on how others misuse their limbs. Sure, some may be kicking your backside, but this attack will project your faith by the way you don't answer back.

You see, nonbelievers are not cancerous to the body; they are just not connected to the body. Your limbs' response to not kick back or punch back may be the answer that keeps the body from cancer. Your projection of mercy as a part of HIS BODY could be the invitation that connects others to HIS BODY.

When you already know you are being body watched, then how you use your limbs should be to serve, not to sever. Are your arms hugging more than your fingers are pointing? Are your hands building people up or are they clenched as you beat them down? Think about something as simple as what your fingers can express without having to say a word. People can read the middle finger's cursing as easily as the thumbs-up blessing. How about using your fingers to text-message Bible verses to your nonbelieving family members, friends or coworkers?

Every one of your limbs can be projecting your faith by connecting to those without faith.

Just as there are many members, yet one body, in Christ, the many members in your body ought to be used to point others to Christ. Your limbs can speak by the way

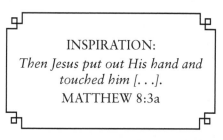

INSPIRATION:
Then Jesus put out His hand and touched him [. . .].
MATTHEW 8:3a

your arms reach and even by the way your hands touch. Your limbs can proclaim by where your legs go and even how your foot holds. A foothold is how you stand bold. **U MAY B THE ONLY BIBLE SOMEBODY READS** is knowing that you may be the limb that saves someone from being in eternal limbo. A genuine reaching out to grab a slipping hand can be the very connection that helps that person stand.

Jesus spoke volumes by not saying a word. He used His hands to wash His disciples' feet, leading by example and showing them how it's possible to project service with how one uses his limbs. With just His hands, Jesus was able to connect everyone to HIS BODY.

Consider sign language and the game of charades! If the body's movements can be legibly read, then let our limbs' language connect others to HIS BODY to be fed. If you ever feel misled as His

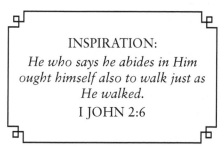

INSPIRATION:
He who says he abides in Him ought himself also to walk just as He walked.
I JOHN 2:6

limb, go to the Gospels and read in red—what Jesus said—and you will find your mobility rightly directed by the Head. As His limb, it's all about Him!

Be legible. Be His limbs.
Be projecting. Be connecting.
Be the Bible!

CHARACTER STAMP:

I MAY B limbs. A person's limbs are arms and legs. Arms can reach out to caress with the hand or help someone get up. Legs can carry the body to the place where one is needed or stand up to stand out from the crowd. Limbs are extremities that can be strategically used as remedies.
Use your life as a limb that pulls another from a state of limbo.
I MAY B limbs.

Reach out willingly to reach out compassionately. Kneel down humbly to stand up strongly.

SCARS

-illustration of the law-

To exercise the law of HIS BODY, be His scars. Be *revealing your healing*.

Every scar has a story to tell, but as His scar you have glory to tell. Jesus wears His scars still, in His glorified body, as evidence to convince doubters like Thomas (John 20:24-29) that He had beaten death and to show us that suffering is absolutely necessary. Furthermore, Jesus' scars are the verification of His humanity, "Son of Man," who, as deity, was able to redeem man—"Son of God."

Jesus' scars are a result of His suffering for you; so when you become His scars, you are committed to suffering for Him. Did you know that the only man-made items in heaven are His scars? However, His scars revealed proclaim, "You are healed."

> INSPIRATION:
> *But He was wounded for our transgressions, He was bruised for our iniquities; the chastisement for our peace was upon Him, and by His stripes we are healed.*
> ISAIAH 53:5

Your scars will be of no value by themselves. Sure you can regale others with war stories about what you have been through, but what about the post-traumatic stress that a wound leaves? With such revealing there is no healing.

Being His scar is telling others about what you have been through—physically, emotionally, spiritually, mentally, relationally—but showing them the proof of your healing. "Scar gazers" will notice the blemish that your skin wears or the mark that your life bears from what you have experienced; but their read can be a mislead, unless your report tells of a legible bleed—the blood shed by Christ on Calvary, which is revealing your healing.

> INSPIRATION:
> *Blessed be the God and Father of our Lord Jesus Christ, the Father of mercies and God of all comfort, Who comforts us in our tribulation, that we may be able to comfort those who are in any trouble, with the comfort with which we ourselves are comforted by God.*
> II CORINTHIANS 1:3-4

People can question our story, but they cannot question scars that tell of greater glory. Expose your scars, and explain God's delivery from that affliction. If it is only blood and the pus of infection that drips forth from your trials and tribulations, then your revealing cannot be appealing. Even your most loving friends will grow weary of your sorrowful tale. Instead, the goal is to show the victory to the Doubting Thomases. Thus, as His scars, you represent healing from guilt and shame, sorrow and disappointment, pain and anguish. With the comfort with which you have been comforted, you will comfort others.

In order for your wounds to heal, the scabs must not be picked or probed. When others attempt to criticize you, harass you, tease you or question you about what you've done or what you've had done to you, your non-response will allow the "scabbing" to have its perfect way and eventually prove healing.

Jesus showed His scars to prove His resurrection, and He now shows His scars to prove His restoration power in our lives. Everybody has scars, but they may not know how to wear them. For many, it tears at them—*Definers; their scars define them.* For some, it scares them—*Confiners; their scars confine them.* For others, it stares at them—*Reminders; their scars remind them.* And because they do not read the Word nor do they know the Healer, you must let them read you by living like you've been healed. Thus, your scars are your *refiners; your scars refine you.*

> INSPIRATION:
> *Then [Jesus] said to Thomas, "Reach your finger here, and look at My hands; and reach your hand here, and put it into My side. Do not be unbelieving, but believing."*
> JOHN 20:27

Being His scars serves as a testimonial of past pain, present healing, and future purpose. You must humbly commit to exposing your scars to this hurting world in order to show them that healing is by God's grace alone. Without sharing your pain, nobody will know your Healer.

Be legible. Be His scars.
Be revealing your healing.
Be the Bible!

CHARACTER STAMP:

I MAY B scars. A scar is a mark left after injured tissue has healed. Scars are permanent reminders of past pain, but evidence of present healing. Big or small, a disfiguring scar can be seen from afar. With a purposeful acceptance of our scars—including emotional, mental, and relational scars—we can turn such messes into messages. Jesus showed His scars to testify to Thomas that it was indeed He who had endured the cross and had risen from the dead. If Jesus used His scars to reveal the healing by faith, so should you!
I MAY B scars.

Expose your scars to express your healing.

ILLEGIBLE

-violation of the law-

"For I know that in me (that is, in my flesh) nothing good dwells [...] O wretched man that I am! Who will deliver me from this body of death?" (Romans 7: 18, 24).

I may have begun with a time when I was legible as HIS BODY, but there were plenty of times when I was illegible. It wasn't that I was just unreadable; in fact, I was vulnerable. Clearly susceptible to irrational response! Thus, it is fitting that I share such examples with you that you may learn from my wretched man and know that delivery is possible for every man. The thought of this illegibility awakens a gamut of emotions in me, but they are all used for the progressive motion in me.

Knowing what I know now about the law of HIS BODY and how to represent the head, which is Christ, I find myself thinking tactically in regards to possibly being the only Bible somebody may read. "How can I use every component of my being—internal and external—to bring people to Christ?" Evangelizing requires strategy as the Holy Spirit works through you to appeal to all walks of life. Jew or Gentile. Male or female. Tatted-up bodies or no tattoos on the body. All are invited to be a part of HIS BODY. That's the beauty upon the law of HIS BODY.

As I expressed in LEGIBLE, it was my tattoos that prompted the New York women to ask about my life, but they were also used to remind me of God's grace in my life. However, in contrast to that story, I must talk about a time when the ink on my skin and the beliefs expressed therein did not line up with my response. Specifically that same memorial tattoo on my ribs, which I had just gotten a few days before the following incident and just three weeks after my brother John passed away. In fact, because of my vulnerability at the time of this situation, the message tattooed on my skin was entirely denied.

So this is where I will begin, letting you know that the Bible we read—like a tattoo on the skin—must be etched into our hearts for it to be read clearly. Thus, it is crucial to understand that the ink on the pages of the Bible only comes alive when it is applied. If the words or verses are just left on the paper when the cover of the Bible closes, we are no better than Satan. He, too, knows the Word of God like a tattoo on the external man, but because he does not submit to the Truth, the ink does not seep through to his inner man. As a result, he devises his own wicked plan for the fall of man.

Like I said, vulnerable!

I know the guise that ink can create as I have been camouflaged by tattoos since I was 18 years of age. Perhaps I was showing off for you the first tattoo I ever got, which is a cross on my arm with Christ pushing up and "strong-arming" the sin of the world. He took the weight of the world for me. For you! But wait! If you watched me long enough, you would see me do contrary to my ink by strong-arming my own way through life, only to add more weight to myself and others around me. Illegible!

Or maybe I would have shown you the Latin phrase "Deo Volente" inked on my inner arm, which means "Lord willing," but moments later I was willing myself as lord. Lord of my own pathetic world. Illegible!

Perhaps you would have seen two angels tatted below the cross of Christ. This scene has the words "Always Thankful" in flowing script between the angels. However, one angel is crying, while the other one is praising. Thus, it is in every season of life that we are to be thankful. Always. I can see this depiction of ink when I look down on my arm, but failure to look up and believe it would only keep me down and defeated. Illegible!

It was my least exposed tattoo on my ribs that exposed so much, as an irrational response that benefited nobody and—even worse—wrongly represented HIS BODY. This etching is a memorial piece for my brother John's life, with Jesus holding him in His arms and Psalm 34:4 in script. Below this picture are John's date of birth, 9/12/77, and his death date, 12/15/05.

Exactly one month after we lost my brother, I was at a friend's house for the last weekend before everyone went back to college after winter break. It was great to see everyone, but looking back now I see how I was still emotionally numb from all that happened prior to the New Year and probably should have avoided such a "loose" gathering.

It was early evening when we started playing beer pong. People were beginning to show up for the get-together. I was in the garage with three of my best friends—Ryan, Brian, and John—when a friendly rivalry of beer pong quickly turned into an argument. Words in jest from all of us were replaced with words that hurt between Ryan and me. A comment made by Ryan about my flesh made me react in my flesh. He said, "You're nothing but a billboard!"

INFLUENCE:
For the Lord dwells in longsuffering, but the devil in anger.
HERMAS, 140 AD

He may not have meant it as I took it, but I had just gotten the memorial piece for my brother on my ribs, my flesh, and I took his comment about being "a billboard" as a personal attack on my devastating loss. My pride was hurt, and I responded in the flesh.

Without hesitation, I flipped the ping-pong table that held several cups of beer as well as a plate of mozzarella sticks and the accompanying marinara sauce. As if in slow motion, the entire bowl of red sauce splattered against Ryan's shirt. With the calamitous noise caused by the crash of the ping-pong table, the garage was soon flooded by the party attendees—running in to see what had happened. Misunderstandings ensued as it appeared that Ryan was covered with blood. His girlfriend threw her beer can at me, which enraged me further.

Ryan and I ended up on the ground, fighting like a pair of bull dogs. In the middle of it all, Brian's ankle was broken as he attempted to break us up. It was pandemonium, and my irrational response had infected everybody. My behavior was a complete contradiction to the law of HIS BODY, where the extremity of my soul became hell's outreach on earth. And neither did it honor the tattoo on my body. The get-together ended promptly after that.

Just like that! A misunderstood comment about my rest-in-peace tattoo piece was the catalyst that made me react selfishly and rip apart everyone else's peace. I may have been vulnerable, but I was clearly illegible!

On that particular day and at that exact moment, I violated the law of HIS BODY. Now I know that the ink needs to be tattooed on the heart for any type of manifestation to start. His Word I

> INFLUENCE:
> First you take the vice, and then the vice takes you. Just like a vise grip, when we attempt to numb our vulnerabilities, we are only squeezing off our responsibilities: to others and ourselves. You see, responsibility is having the ability to respond judiciously. Practical Insight: When feeling vulnerable, drink deeply of the Bible not the bottle.
> MATTHEW MAHER, 1984-

have tattooed on my heart, that I might not sin against Him (Psalm 119:11, translation mine). My friends and I eventually made up and grew even closer in our relational bond because of this altercation. But it came at the expense of my testimony—even the temporary death of it—until it could be used today for Christ.

"Who will deliver me from this body of death?" (Romans 7:24). "I thank God—through Jesus Christ our Lord!" (v. 25).

VISION RESTORED

You may not have X-ray vision, but God does. He looks into the depths of the heart to search it and test it. Therefore, like David, you must be open to His X-ray vision and pray, "Search me, O God, and know my heart; try me, and know my anxieties; and see if there is any wicked way in me, and lead me in the way everlasting" (Psalm 139:23-24). *As a result, because your "I" is open and transparent to His eye, you can be led to help someone else's sty. You are His body; therefore, focus on seeing yourself and others through Calvary's lens. Not cross-eyed, but straight by the eye of the cross.*
U MAY B HIS BODY!

Crucify self to clarify Christ.

PART XI

---

the law of HIS CHILD

"The foundation of faith's influence is childlike dependence."

appropriating the law:

Biblical influence is humble. You know you are His child when your "I"ndependence becomes faithfully dependent on Him. You cannot begin your day without checking in with Abba Father. Why? Because you are well aware of your vulnerability; thus, you give your Father your cares and burdens, making them His responsibility. This is faith's influence: When you recognize that your Father in heaven cares infinitely for your "I" and only wants to provide adequately for you, then you can begin to demonstrate your childlike dependence. As you receive the Father's care, your "I" must be clearly aware that His only begotten Son Jesus is right there.
U MAY B HIS CHILD!

The antidote to your independent obstinacy is to cultivate childlike dependency.

~seeing the law is being the law~

LEGIBLE

-application of the law-

"Assuredly, I say to you, unless you are converted and become as little children, you will by no means enter the kingdom of heaven" (Matthew 18:3).

When projecting the law of HIS CHILD, we are to be a legible representation of the *character*, *conduct*, and *conversation* of Jesus Christ.

Listen to Jesus' invitation: *"But Jesus said, 'Let the little children come to Me, and do not forbid them; for of such is the kingdom of heaven'" (Matthew 19:14).* But that's not all He said—He instructs "grown-ups" in how to walk as HIS CHILD despite their "mature" age. He said, *"Therefore whoever humbles himself as this little child is the greatest in the kingdom of heaven" (Matthew 18:4).* Yes! We naturally grow into adulthood, but spiritually we must remain like children—not childish, but childlike in faith.

How do we do that? It's not complicated! In fact, consider these words from Jesus, which is the most simplistic, yet intrinsic, instruction for us to begin the process of conversion to grow in the law of HIS CHILD: *"Assuredly, I say to you, unless you are converted and become as little children, you will by no means enter the kingdom of heaven" (Matthew 18:2).*

Not only are we to bring our children to Jesus, but we are to allow the child within us to meet Jesus. Going to Jesus and spending time with Him will multiply our faith by teaching us childlike dependence upon Him as we observe the way He demonstrated trust in His Father. He develops that crucial quality within us, when we cultivate Him within us. When we are in Christ, we become children to God, our heavenly Father. However, we often become too "grown-up" for our own good, and such an independent attitude keeps us away from Jesus and keeps us estranged from the Father.

Wait! I know what you're saying about being legible as HIS CHILD, but shouldn't we still be serious in our demeanor, superior in our thought process, and senior in our dignity? Wrong! Jesus implored us to humble ourselves like a little child, so essentially he wants us to be simple, sensitive, sincere, and even silly.

In other words, we are to be blameless, innocent, and humble when it comes to trusting God. Like a little child who is fully dependent upon his parents, so too must we trust the Lord with our entire being and in all our ways. Growing in the law of HIS CHILD is allowing others to see your childlike dependence and disposition—faith's influence—and introducing them to your Daddy through your big Brother's example. That's right! Being the only Bible somebody may read isn't supposed to be child-proof—it's supposed to be child-proved.

INFLUENCE:

If the devil can get you to fear, he can get you to fail. Fight the feeling of fear by surrendering to the fact of faith. Faith says what God says. And God says, "If I am for you, who can be against you?" Practical Insight: If you did it, own up to it. Then turn it over to God and let Him reweave what you've sewn wrong.

MATTHEW MAHER, 1984-

The word "dynamic" would best describe the surface events that surrounded my circumstances before prison. From March 7, 2009, the day of the accident, until January 7, 2010, the day of sentencing, my situation was speculated about, conjectured against, and assumed arbitrarily in regards to special favor and treatment because of my father's stature in law enforcement and my status in professional sport.

In our local newspaper especially—both in print and online—many people spewed their skewered notions through a column called "Spout Off," which enabled them to make their false and contradictory statements anonymously. While cloaked in darkness, they claimed I would get off lightly because my father was a retired chief of police and currently served as executive undersheriff of the county. The pressure and attention around my senseless crime was indeed dynamic. I deserved the shame, but that did not mean I had to buy into the hate and hostility that motivated the comments.

One particularly nasty "spout off" remains with me to this day: "Bubba is gonna have a Kixx of a good time with Maher in prison." The unknown poster cleverly played on the word "Kixx," the name of the professional soccer team out of Philadelphia for which I was playing at the time of the fatal accident. Though most thought I would get special treatment and others wished I would get brutal treatment, none of them knew that what was actually going on with my situation was how it was being faithfully treated—while the haters were predicting, we were praying!

We, as a family, prayed ceaselessly to our Father in Heaven through the ensuing months. We prayed for the victim's family, for my family, and for my response to what I had done. I prayed personally for God to use my circumstances as He willed, and I asked for the will to no longer fight His desire to have my utmost attention on Him. He heard me.

You see, I know I was HIS CHILD, but I lived my life independent of God—like the prodigal son (Luke 15:11), I believed I could do life on my own. Until my own "pig pen" experience brought me back to myself and pushed me to passionately repent my way back to the Father. And like the prodigal son: God

INFLUENCE:

No one can believe how powerful prayer is and what it can effect, except those who have learned it by experience. It is important when we have a need to go to God in prayer. I know, whenever I have prayed earnestly, that I have been heard and have obtained more than I prayed for. God sometimes delays, but He always comes.

MARTIN LUTHER, 1483-1546

not only received me back, but He met me halfway with open arms of compassion. *"And he arose and came to his father. But when he was still a great way off, his father saw him and had compassion, and ran and fell on his neck and kissed him"* *(Luke 15:20).*

Besides the faith factor, those who cared about the "dynamics" of my situation failed to understand another sharp factor. You see, my situation was a two-edged sword in the eyes of the prosecution. That team had to deal with the dynamics of my family's reputation and my position, which placed my case in the public spotlight, and they were therefore especially careful not to show partiality of any sort. What the public believed was an advantage for me was actually far from it. Consequently, the rug was pulled out from under me as opposed to the matter getting swept under the rug, as many surmised.

Truthfully, I would not have accepted any favoritism had it been offered, which explains why seven months after the accident I pleaded guilty to the highest charge possible: first-degree aggravated manslaughter, a charge that held a possible sentence of 10-to-30 years. I felt helpless but not hopeless, and this is exactly where God our Father wants His children to be—fully dependent upon Him no matter our circumstances. That's the maturity behind the law of HIS CHILD.

Ironically, the haters were concerned about who my father was, thinking I would get off, but the true insight concerning the spiritual dynamics beneath the surface dynamics was Who my Daddy is! Abba Father. At the time of this writing, I have been incarcerated for over four years, and my life is evidence that as HIS CHILD, He works all things out for good, making them legible, to those who love Him and to those who are called according to His purpose (Romans 8:28, translation mine).

Please do not misunderstand: God never endorses our wrong-doing; however, the moment we repent and return to Him, He takes us back and uses our adversity to bring Himself glory. I deserve nothing because of what I did, but God the Father has given me everything because of what His Son did.

I now see clearly how my family's dependence upon God has allowed God the Father to bestow His grace and mercy to all of us, His children. *"No good thing will He withhold from those who walk uprightly" (Psalm 84:11).*

SENSITIVE

-illustration of the law-

To grow in the law of HIS CHILD, be sensitive. Be *stimulated by sympathy.*

Consider this! Nobody cares what you know until they know that you care. Thus, one must be considerate of others in order to be seen as "Bible-literate" by others. Even if the recipients of your sensitive ministering do not read the Bible, they will be reading you. A child of God must have the *DNA* of the Father, the Son, and the Holy Spirit. This (D)ivine (N)ature (A)ctivated in you enables you to do the will of the Father because you—like Jesus, the Son—are stimulated by sympathy in the Holy Spirit.

> INSPIRATION:
> *Be kindly affectionate to one another with brotherly love, in honor giving preference to one another; not lagging in diligence, fervent in spirit, serving the Lord; rejoicing in hope, patient in tribulation, continuing steadfastly in prayer; distributing to the needs of the saints, given to hospitality. Rejoice with those who rejoice, and weep with those who weep.*
> ROMANS 12:10-15

Sometimes children on the playground cry because another child fell. The scrape they see on their playmate can inspire wails and tears all around. In the same way, we cry with others who have experienced that painful "fall." I'm not talking about joining the company of misery or inviting yourself to someone else's pity party, but being a shoulder to cry on for those who are going through it.

Showing them that you care is a prerequisite to showing them what you know about the One who can take their cares!

Being sensitive doesn't necessarily mean you understand someone else's struggles, but it shows them that you care for them through their struggle and in spite of their struggle. Flipping to the dictionary under D, we find a list that provides more than enough reasons to be sensitive to others going through their dilemmas—death, disease, destruction, divorce, depression, discouragement, doubt, darkness, debt, distress. As you allow your sensitivity to precede you, a child of God is how they'll read you.

On the flipside of the D's, you must be sensitive to other people's needs. These are not always dilemmas; but when you show someone that you care by catering to their needs, you allow your *DNA* to open up the Bible to them through the expression of one word—love. Often, a group of children will laugh together for no reason—their merriment is contagious! Now that's sensitivity in action! It is not being *touchy* in emotions, but being *in touch* with one's emotions. Jesus moved with such childlike sympathy that sinners were not only attracted to Him, they were comfortable around Him. He was in complete control of His emotions, yet He was still able to be in harmony with their emotions. Legible.

There is something about aging that diminishes our childlike sensitivity, but there is no reason for a defensive guard to go up. Indifference and callousness block our affections from stimulation and the beautiful reason that God gave us feelings in the first

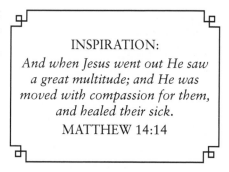

INSPIRATION:
And when Jesus went out He saw a great multitude; and He was moved with compassion for them, and healed their sick.
MATTHEW 14:14

place—to feel and help heal. Thus, in order to penetrate a nonbeliever's emotional wall, yours must come down first.

As HIS CHILD, God desires that we ache with other people's sorrow and rejoice with other people's happiness. The sensitivity of a little child can melt the oldest and coldest heart; so, too, should a child of God be able to minister to another person's heart with child-proved sympathy. Now that's maturity! Let us not lose that childlike innocence. Let us use our childlike faith by tapping into our *DNA*.

> *Be legible. Be sensitive.*
> *Be stimulated by sympathy.*
> *Be the Bible!*

CHARACTER STAMP:

I MAY B sensitive. Sensitivity is connectivity. It is a response to stimulation, and as His child, sensitivity must move you toward consolation. When one child sees another child crying, he or she will usually join in on the cause—not even knowing the cause. Likewise when the stimulus is joyful laughter. When your sensory capacity is lined up with your spiritual receptivity, you will move into the realm of compassionate ministry. Therefore, be sensible of feelings that you may help others with healing.
I MAY B *sensitive.*

Ministering to the slightest of emotions can have the greatest impression.

SIMPLE

-illustration of the law-

To grow in the law of HIS CHILD, be simple. Be *profoundly simple and simply profound.*

"KISS me, I'm Christian!" Not so fast, though, because I'm not talking about an intimate kiss, but an intellectual kiss. One that reminds you to (K)eep (I)t (S)imply (S)imple! We so easily overcomplicate life, instead of easily conquering life. When the parents tell their children that they are going to Disney World, the kids don't worry about how this trip is going to happen financially or logistically, they simply trust positionally—because Mom and Dad said it, the kids purely believe it. So, too, must you take God at His Word.

Being simple like a child has nothing to do with gullibility and everything to do with expectancy. When you incorporate this profoundly simple mindset as HIS CHILD, you get simply profound results by your faith. You expect mir-

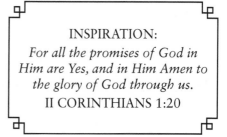

INSPIRATION:
For all the promises of God in Him are Yes, and in Him Amen to the glory of God through us.
II CORINTHIANS 1:20

acles in your life because God's Word cannot return to Him void; He does not make empty promises—He has the power to see them through to completion. You don't have to analyze or hypothesize. No! You can trust that what Abba Father said will be accomplished in His perfect timing, and always for your good and His glory. Furthermore, God does not always explain.

As HIS CHILD, it is important to remain simplistic in your faith, keeping it simply simple—KISS—as you take and apply the Bible's words from God's lips. The "adults" of this world will be amazed at your ability to conduct yourself through complex situations with joy. There is no reason to concern yourself with things that may be too difficult to understand; (K)eeping (I)t (S)imply (S)imple is knowing that it's all in your Father's perfect plan. And that's sufficient. You're not crying like a baby through it nor are you worrying like an adult because of it. You are simply trusting in spite of it!

> INSPIRATION:
> *Surely I have calmed and quieted my soul, like a weaned child with his mother;like a weaned child is my soul within me.*
> PSALM 131:2

"It can't be that simple," our mature and logical mind will reason and argue. But as HIS CHILD, we know that Jesus has already overcome the complications and tribulations of the world. He reminds us to KISS and recall: in Him we have peace, and we can be of good cheer no matter what we are facing (John 16:33). Now that's simple! Biblically simple!

Nobody is going to want salvation if it seems too hard or complicated. This is a major problem today as religions have falsely confused the straightforward gospel. We need to take the faith of the Bible back and live it out for the world to see how simple Christ has made it for us. There are not a million ways to God; just one way—Jesus.

Think of all the "adults" who don't even know they could be God's children because the rest of God's children have not shown them how to be His children by simply accepting His Son. Tell others about the Savior: *"For God so loved the world that He gave His only begotten Son, that whoever believes in Him should not perish but have everlasting life" (John 3:16).* To make a potential child of God able to see the Bible, it takes a child of God to be the Bible.

> INSPIRATION:
> *The law of the Lord is perfect, converting the soul; the testimony of the Lord is sure, making wise the simple.*
> PSALM 19:7

The truths that make you legible are profoundly simple and simply profound. There need not be a grand formula or scientific equation to complicate kindergarten kindness. Tell the world's people they are loved, and let them know how much Abba Father suffered and sacrificed to show them His love. Teach others how easy it is by the way you KISS. *"Draw near to God, and He will draw near to you" (James 4:8a),* and then He will draw others through you!

Be legible. Be simple.
Be profoundly simple. Be simply profound.
Be the Bible!

CHARACTER STAMP:

I MAY B simple. Simple in this respect is not a lack of education. To be simple like a child is to refrain from dwelling on complications. Simplicity is having an awareness of clarity—a characteristic that allows for unclouded decisions because your frame of reference originates from a humble position.
Simplicity is surety and shows great maturity.
I MAY B simple.

To be extraordinarily uncomplicated is child's play.

SINCERE

-illustration of the law-

To grow in the law of HIS CHILD, be sincere. Be *genuinely real and really genuine.*

You can be sincere—and sincerely wrong! Since **U MAY B THE ONLY BIBLE SOMEBODY READS,** it's important to be sincerely right when it comes to the "text" that you put out to be read. You have a valuable part to play when it comes to reaching your nonbelieving friends, family, and, yes, even your foes. But none of them will hear you if they sense there's nothing sincere in you.

Therefore, as HIS CHILD who knows the Truth, you must be able to handle it with sincere love—truth and love. If you tell others the truth without love, that's brutality. If you show love to others without truth, that's hypocrisy. The goal is to be sincere in what you say and do, even to the point of saying the darndest things. *Kids Say the Darndest Things* was a TV show hosted by Bill Cosby in the 1990s and was based on a conception originally made popular 50 years earlier on television and in books by Art Linkletter. In response to questions about life, kids gave sincere answers with typically hilarious results. The children were being genuinely real and really genuine, and they touched our hearts by speaking theirs.

> INSPIRATION:
> *Now the purpose of the commandment is love from a pure heart, from a good conscience, and from sincere faith.*
> I TIMOTHY 1:5

Now translate that same childlike sincerity to the gospel, and imagine how it would be more effective if it were delivered with truth and love. Not telling people, "You're going to hell if you don't accept Jesus' love"; rather, telling them they are spared from hell because of Jesus' love. It may be the darndest thing for you to say, but it's also the sincerest thing to relay. Caring about a person's eternal salvation is no small issue, and that is why the discussion must be administered from a child-like concern that is sincere, genuine, and honest.

Being a child of the Most High allows you to live at such liberty that your presence around others is never strained or strange. Just really genuine. You are able to move with the perfect blend of truth and love, with words and deeds that point to your Savior. Even if your faith is misunderstood, your sincerity is unquestioned. They may wonder about your motives, but by your authentic representation of Christ they will eventually acknowledge that you are a child of God.

> INSPIRATION:
> *For our boasting is this: the testimony of our conscience that we conducted ourselves in the world in simplicity and godly sincerity, not with fleshly wisdom but by the grace of God, and more abundantly toward you.*
> II CORINTHIANS 1:12

The world will read you—that's a guarantee. What will they believe you to be by the example that they see? One who is sincere? Or one who points out their sin when you come near?

Be legible. Be sincere.
Be genuinely real. Be really genuine.
Be the Bible!

CHARACTER STAMP:

I MAY B sincere. When a person is sincere, he or she is genuine and real. A child is free of hypocrisy because he has not yet been swayed by life's democracy—the rule of the majority. Sincerity is honesty. When you can learn to say what you mean and mean what you say—in truth and love—then your testimony will be received as authentic. Take on the sincerity of the Bible.
I MAY B *sincere.*

Truth + Love = Integrity

SILLY

-illustration of the law-

To grow in the law of HIS CHILD, be silly. Be *soliciting silliness*.

Let's get straight to the laughter of the matter! Like a child, we are to be silly-dilly, holly-jolly when it comes to our eternal inheritance. Heaven! That thought alone ought to ensure that we are the most joyful people on earth. By faith in Jesus Christ, you are now relationally a child of God, and you have the Spirit of His Son in your heart crying out, "Abba, Father!" Thus, you are now a child; and if a child, then an heir of God through Christ. This is a celebratory matter, for you are no longer a slave to sin, but a solicitor of silliness—rejoicing in life here because you have an eternal hereafter.

Children are free to be silly as a result of being stress-free. Think about it! When was the last time you saw a child stressed out or anxious about tomorrow? Why then does the world see you, as HIS CHILD, worried? A child can play and laugh throughout the day because he knows Mommy and Daddy have everything taken care of—no matter what. Such trusting innocence is maturity, yet we see children and their silliness as immaturity. It ought not to be so because our Heavenly Father promises that everything is taken care of as well; He wants us to "laugh and

> INSPIRATION:
> *In hope of eternal life which God, who cannot lie, promised before time began.*
> TITUS 1:2

play" our way through the day. *"Rejoice in the Lord always. Again I will say, rejoice!" (Philippians 4:4).*

Your laughter is the joyful attitude of your heart, which is heard in your conversation. Your play is your productivity, which is seen in your conduct's liberty. Therefore, "laugh and play" is the sum of your heart's character, which must be solicited for the world to see that others may buy into your difference. And your difference is your Abba Father's providence and protection. *"Do not sorrow, for the joy of the Lord is your strength" (Nehemiah 8:10b).*

INSPIRATION:
For our light affliction, which is but for a moment, is working for us a far more exceeding and eternal weight of glory.
II CORINTHIANS 4:17

You can be silly as an adult because you are still a child. Of course, some of life's experiences aren't laughing matters, but all of life's experiences are temporary matters in light of eternity—making the momentary affliction "silly" in comparison to the eternal weight of glory. People need to read the Bible's theme through you! And that theme is the hope of heaven through Christ. The hope of heaven through life. The hope of heaven through strife. Recognizing that the hope of heaven is an actual site. You need to live with the hope of heaven in sight.

Soliciting silliness is living enveloped by this hope, which enables others to see heaven even as you go through hell! If a child can find reassurance in hearing his father say, "Everything is going to be OK," then why are we deaf to this concrete truth from our Heavenly Father?

You are HIS CHILD, and you can be silly in spite of your age or circumstances. Silliness is not foolishness—it's lightheartedness. It is having the understanding that your Father has everything under control even when things seem out of control.

Thus, you can be seen rejoicing through various trials because your faith is being purified. You know this, now you must show this. In a world filled with so much pain, let the world see the Word as you successfully suffer through your pain.

Be legible. Be silly.
Be soliciting silliness.
Be the Bible!

CHARACTER STAMP:

I MAY B silly. Silly is what silly does, but childlike silliness is an openness to the wonders of the world. It is retaining the ability to be amazed by the supernatural. Children can be most silly when awaiting a Christmas surprise; similar to the exhilaration of this experience is how you must be silly when it comes to God's miraculous gifts. Reignite that silliness within you as you begin to see God's fullness all around you.
I MAY B silly.

Alleviate life's pressure with grateful gaiety.

ILLEGIBLE

-violation of the law-

*"[Y]ou once walked according to the course of this world
[...] among whom also we all once conducted ourselves in the
lusts of our flesh, fulfilling the desires of the flesh and mind,
and were by nature children of wrath, just as the others"*
(Ephesians 2: 2-3).

I may have begun with a time when I was legible as HIS CHILD, but there were plenty of times when I was illegible. It wasn't that I was just unreadable; in fact, I was visibly readable. Clearly publicized! Thus, it is fitting that I share this lifestyle with you so that ...

I grew up in a Christian household with my mother and father, who shared a strong faith in God and who were well-known throughout our community. My father was in law enforcement, and my mother was a stay-at-home mom devoted to raising her children in the Lord. Inside church and outside church, I learned from an early age the lifestyle of integrity by initiative and accountability by action.

My parents modeled an upstanding lifestyle for my three older brothers and me. They practiced daily devotions to God and doing service to their neighbors. They taught us godly values and morals and showed us by example. They didn't beat it into us—they built it into us.

From an early age, I demonstrated an aptitude for excellence in athletics and academics. I felt very blessed because I was also competitive, and my abilities placed me years ahead of my peers. I was on a trajectory toward certain success in any sport of my choice.

In the company of my family, I attended church regularly and was a member of Christian youth groups and Sunday school classes. I also attended Christian school from first- to eighth-grade and was a member of a number of extracurricular activities. In virtually every group, I was the captain or president—a natural-born leader. I spoke out openly about my faith, even in my public high school.

My mother was a co-creator and educator for a government-funded abstinence program titled, "Peer Challenge." I participated in "Peer Challenge," giving speeches that encouraged other teens to practice abstinence from risky behaviors. I even did a TV commercial that promoted this stance.

At the same time, I was busy making every type of All-Star team for soccer. I played in the Olympic Development Program as one of 22 kids to represent the state of New Jersey from the East Coast. My achievements in basketball were equally consistent and constantly publicized in the media.

Additionally, I was class president my sophomore year, and Bible Club president my junior and senior years. I ranked in the top 10 percent of my class academically. I excelled and excelled some more, with a paper trail to prove it.

I received a full scholarship to Temple University in Philadelphia, where I repeated the cycle of excellence. I made the Division 1 Atlantic 10 Conference All-Rookie Team as a freshman. I was captain as a junior and senior, and there were other accolades. Eventually I was drafted as a first-round pick to play pro. In all this limelight, I was still on track in the class-light—maintaining a 3.0, and above grade-point average in my major. I graduated from Temple's Fox School of Business with a Bachelor of Science in Business Administration and a concentration in Legal Studies.

I got myself an elite degree that I did not need in order to pursue my career of choice. This was because of the athletic pedigree that allowed me to follow in my older brother Anthony's footsteps, who was already playing professional soccer at that point. But before I jump ahead to my lifestyle as a pro athlete, it's important to know that I was involved in Christian extracurricular organizations in college as well. I helped start a Fellowship of Christian Athletes (FCA) on Temple's campus and was also part of Campus Crusades for Christ.

As a pro soccer player, my performance as a rookie allotted me starting positions on my first two teams. First, with the Carolina Railhawks of the United Soccer Leagues First Division, where my first starting game was against world powerhouse Cruz Azul of the Mexican First Division. This game was played in front of over 30,000 fans. Following this season, I honored the Major Indoor Soccer League (MISL) player draft by signing with the New Jersey Ironmen. They drafted me as the first pick ever in the franchise's history—first round, second pick overall. I played alongside USA soccer legend and multiple World Cup participant Tony Meola. Tony and I became good friends off the field because of our commonality of faith. Once again, I was part of FCA as a pro and even had my own Athletes in Action (AIA) player card that helped make me a fan favorite in New Jersey. I was also able to meet and take pictures with world soccer great Pele', as he was the honorary captain for our home opener in the Prudential Center in Newark. That game was attended by over 17,000 fans. While on this team, I was among those invited to New York's Time's Square to ring the closing ball on NASDAQ.

This is a brief summation of a life that many people would have desired. Success. Fame. Wealth. Brains and brawn. And, according to my mom, good looks and charm. I was "that guy!" But now let me conclude my opening paragraph:

Thus, it is fitting that I share this lifestyle with you so that you can see how even through all of the accolades and accomplishments, passions and possessions, I was still ILLEGIBLE! None of my worldly pursuits were used for godly purposes. Sure, they may have come off that way on the external view, but that's the major problem. The internal was off, in spite of everyone believing it was on. I thought I was a self-made man, breaking through each level of success on my own. That belief does nothing but bring one to an inevitable breaking point.

"Pride goes before destruction, and a haughty spirit before a fall" (Proverbs 16:18).

Though I was not always illegible in that lifestyle as HIS CHILD, I did enough in my independent living to put out a confusing version of the Bible that I said I represented. But here is the promise! Though I may not have been seen by man as HIS CHILD at times or even if I fooled others into seeing me as HIS CHILD at other times, God still saw me as HIS CHILD all the time. Even when I was living for myself—violation of the law—it was ultimately leading me back to Him to learn the application of the law! And that's the promise within the law of HIS CHILD.

> INFLUENCE:
> *The violation of this law will eventually lead to the application of the law. Because as HIS CHILD, God will finish what He started in you. As Pastor Rick Warren once wrote, "When you're going through the motions spiritually, don't be surprised when God allows pain into your life. Pain is the fuel of passion." Practical Insight: Man's greatest need is God's greatest deed: FORGIVENESS. Accept it!*
> MATTHEW MAHER, 1984-

> INFLUENCE:
> *I will not glory because I am righteous, but because I am redeemed; not because I am clear of sin, but because my sins are forgiven.*
> AMBROSE of MILAN, 340-397 AD

So I humbly publicize my past in order to glorify God for what He has done in my present. Illegible then to be legible now! As Paul said confidently about his faith, *"Imitate me, just as I also imitate Christ"* (*I Corinthians 11:1*), I say, *"Read* me now, as I follow Christ!"

VISION RESTORED

Envisioning yourself as His child is not a daunting pursuit. In fact, it is God Most High who desires to pursue you. He sent His Son Jesus into this world to illuminate sight that was blinded by sin. When you confess with your mouth and believe in your heart that Jesus died for your sins and rose on the third day from the tombsite, then you are adopted as His child and receive spiritual new sight.
U MAY B HIS CHILD!

See farther by drawing nearer.

CONCLUSION

I saved my thesis statement for the very end, not because it's not important, but because it's of utmost importance. I want the title, this accountability line, to do more than stick; I desire for it to penetrate your soul. You see, this book—my thesis statement—has not been a proposition just to help initiate a general idea; it has been a revelation that should help instigate biblical ideals. There needs to be a standard of excellence—God's Law—for us to be trained by, yet we are not using the Bible as our trainer to learn God's Law as we should. His Law is liberty in Christ, and that is why He sent His only begotten Son to demonstrate this liberty in life.

Jesus said, *"A disciple is not above his teacher, but everyone who is perfectly trained will be like his teacher"* (Luke 6:40).

In other words, **U MAY B THE ONLY BIBLE SOMEBODY READS** is about having your "pages" point to the Savior, Who is the Trainer and Teacher. But without having His Word—Christ—as the standard in your heart/mind/soul, there can be no power in your godly influence. Without the Word in your heart, life cannot be abundantly lived. Life cannot be legibly read. Life cannot be life. It is living dead.

The truth be told, this book's title came to me long ago. As mentioned in the preface, it was my mom's way of reminding me to remain steadfast in my faith and true to my conviction. So when I found myself in a prison of my own making, it was my mother's voice that encouraged me to cultivate the Word within me, to allow it to be read outside of me. The monumental difference between back then, when she used to say those words to me, and how they have impacted me now is that I've allowed them to take root. Those words are no longer just felt on the surface, but now they have fastened me to purpose.

When I first wrote this book's title down on paper, I had no idea in what direction I wanted to take the concept. But God knew. One day, a friend asked me if I had ever read Robert Greene's *The 48 Laws of Power*, a book that is very popular behind these walls. I had heard of it, but I had never read it. After he explained its theme, I was curious to see its content. So I began reviewing it.

Meanwhile, I had already written the preface of this book, but I was frozen in which direction to go after that—until I read Greene's book. As I prayerfully made it through that book, the direction for this book dawned upon me. In *The 48 Laws of Power*, the author painstakingly equips minds to win the contest of power by any means necessary. Greene's laws advise and instruct on the art of deception.

In Greene's own words, which appear in his preface, "We need to be subtle—congenial yet cunning, democratic yet devious. This game of constant duplicity most resembles the power dynamic that existed in the scheming world of the old aristocratic court."

Chapter by chapter, Greene's handbook for acquiring power teaches his disciples how to get ahead in the world at the soul's expense. Sadly, Greene's concepts are not unique—his theme is repeated in many other texts and by numerous other philosophers and ideologues. So, why can't we, as disciples of Christ, have an instructional text that reminds us of our power—Christ in us—that reaches others for salvation? A text with practical guidance on how to be a legible representation of the *character*, *conduct*, and *conversation* of Jesus Christ. And a text with biblical backing that teaches how to discern and leverage influence with the deployment of 11 unique laws that promote infectious faith and contagious example.

I have read so much material and have discovered that there are not many Christian books that teach how to influence the nonbeliever. The media—television, radio, films, Internet, print publications, and music—certainly propagate secular culture and teach us about their hellish "kingdom" here on earth, so where are the biblical vehicles that teach us about the inspiration we have from heaven's kingdom on earth? It is time to take back that power and use it not to manipulate, but to instigate for integrity. Influence for Christ.

John "Little John" Paladino is a former mob enforcer who lived his life based on *The 48 Laws of Power*, yet look what happened when man's "laws" of power met God's power (see Foreword). Holy Spirit transformation—an about-face. Little John's life has changed. He now perceives the power of God in his life, and he knows that he may be the only Bible somebody reads, which impacts how he lives each moment of each day.

Ultimately, this book was written because I recognized that this life is a battle for souls, not a battle for worldly wealth and power. Since the war has already been won at Calvary, granting us victory in Christ, the battle we wage is not outward, but inward. It's personal. The conscious thought strategy that a Christian needs to know is realizing that you are always being watched.

Personally, since I knew as a celebrity that I was always being watched, the challenge wasn't for me to prove to others that I was different. The challenge was to simply live life already proven in Christ to make a difference. I didn't take advantage of anyone in this process. I didn't conceal my intentions. I didn't play on anyone's emotions. I didn't stir up any waters to catch fish. I didn't pose as a friend or work as a spy.

No! I simply learned that you must be confident in your maturity in Him, where this presentation of faith and representation of Christ is the attraction that can lead others in the right direction—in the opposite direction from where they were headed. Now that's power from on high.

The world may have *The 48 Laws of Power* in one book, but we have 66 books of power in one law—God's Law. His Word. Christ. The standard. The Bible is made up of 66 books of divine power that is *"able to do exceedingly abundantly above all that we ask or think, according to the power that works in us"* *(Ephesians 3:20)*. But the power must get *in* us, and that power is only activated when you allow Christ to dwell in your heart by faith.

That is the point of life! That God sent HIS WORD to this earth. A virgin birth to be pure from sin. Born without sin. Lived without sin. The perfect Lamb of God. His power. Jesus the Word in the flesh. He came that all men may be saved by accepting the Word in the flesh, reading the Word in the mind, and living the Word in the Spirit. Not adherence to the letter of man's "laws," but obedience to the Spirit of God's Law in man!

U MAY B THE ONLY BIBLE SOMEBODY READS.

Just as Christ was sent to be read, so are we. But how are we being read? There will always be misinterpretations and different translations, but God's Word never returns void. Many misread the Word and many will misread you, but how are you living to be read—or bluntly, what's in you?

I know very well the book of my past and what I showed off on my "cover," but my inside pages were filled with the wrong message. They were filled with my own messages and my own themes. I want to be read differently these days because it is no longer my own word or power I live on, but the *"Word [which] became flesh and dwelt among us, and we beheld His glory, the glory as of the only begotten of the Father, full of grace and truth" (John 1:14).* Grace to appeal and truth to reveal. When I say "read me now," it is a challenge to myself—that I show Christ in my flesh and have the Word read in my actions. Friend, I get it now. I finally understand why my soul was allowed to live on the night of March 7, 2009. And I now desire to inspire those who read me as well as inspire you who read this book. Ultimately that God may equip all of us to be read for His glory as we inspire others.

This book may have been written from prison, but without God's Word and His power in my life, living is prison. I challenge you to take God's "66 Books of Power"—the Bible—and learn His Law by trusting in Him through Christ. Galatians 3:24 states, *"Therefore the law was our tutor to bring us to Christ, that we might be justified by faith."* Likewise by faith, let the 11 unique laws in this book become your tutor to help bring Christ out of you. Every believer has been ordained to influence, for God has made us minsters of the law of Christ:

To project *love*, to reflect *light*, to connect *life*.

Finally: *"Not that we are sufficient of ourselves to think of anything as being from ourselves, but our sufficiency is from God, who also made us sufficient as ministers of the new covenant, not of the letter but of the Spirit; for the letter kills, but the Spirit gives life" (II Corinthians 3: 5-6).*

Now that's power! And His power is in you when Christ is in you: *"Christ the power of God and the wisdom of God" (I Corinthians 1:24b).* Even the wisest and strongest vehicles that the world uses are powerless *"because the foolishness of God is wiser than men, and the weakness of God is stronger than men" (v. 25).*

Friend, now you are ready to take the **U MAY B** Challenge. You may even be courageous enough to invite a friend as you leverage your influence with godliness. I implore you to work this book as a workbook in order to inspire you to get into the Good Book. Look up the INSPIRATION verses highlighted at the end of the chapters. Learn from the INFLUENCE wielded by the great minds of the grateful men whose quotes from their experiences in bygone times deepen our faith today.

IT STARTS NOW ...

APPENDIX

The *U MAY B* Challenge & Contract

The **I MAY B** movement starts now! Join it and share it! But first and foremost, learn to be it by heeding it when you read it. It's never too late to begin reading the Bible. No age disqualifies you, neither does experience nor education nullify you. Why read the Bible? Because **U MAY B THE ONLY BIBLE SOME-BODY READS.**

"Where there is no vision (or revelation), the people perish; but he that keepeth the law, happy is he" *(Proverbs 29:18, KJV)*. Our hope is cultivated in the Word, therefore we must get in the Word. My challenge for any who have read this book is to begin increasing your time spent in the Bible. If your time spent in God's Word is zero, start with 10 minutes a day. If you are accustomed to 10 minutes a day, ante up to 30 minutes and so forth. Replace some of your TV time or video time or social media time with Bible time. The purpose of the **U MAY B** challenge is to elevate your faith and generate hope in your life.

Make it personal as the **U MAY B** challenge turns into an **I MAY B** charge! Personally, when I realized that **I MAY B** the only Bible some of my peers may ever read, I began to take ownership of my influence as it is stirred up by reading the Bible. I learned that I must read in order to be read.

Finally, I find that **I MAY B** hope for those around me. **I MAY B** inspiration for life. **I MAY B** responsible, accountable, presentable, so I must be legible. **I MAY B** comfort. **I MAY B** direction. **I MAY B** _____. Fill in the blank, and know that **U MAY B THE ONLY BIBLE SOMEBODY READS.**

It begins with you! If you are serious about Jesus, the movement of the Spirit of God desires to partner with you to move the world. It's time to revolutionize the people around us by inspiring hope in the heavens above us.

Friend, if you are about your Father's business like Jesus, then after this private **U MAY B** Challenge, you become a public **I MAY B** Influencer. Private sacrifice equals public success.

Turn your hour of desperation into an hour of revelation. Dare to become an **I MAY B** Influencer wherever God has planted you. Whether in a prison or a palace, be worthy to be read. Now, share this with a friend.

I MAY B one person …
And **U MAY B** one person …
But together we may be **ONE MOVEMENT!**

The **BIBLE REVIVAL** begins inside of **U!**

ACCOUNTABILITY CONTRACT

I, _____, pledge to increase my Bible reading time, knowing that it's not about perfection, but progression. I admit that without the Bible in me, the Bible cannot be read from me. Also, without hope, my vision is skewed and my mission is crippled. Therefore, I'll begin reading the Word of God today that **I MAY B** enthusiastic about my God-given purpose and about my tomorrow. I humbly accept the challenge that **I MAY B THE ONLY BIBLE SOMEBODY READS.**

Signed:

Date_____

IF YOU ENJOYED THIS BOOK, WILL YOU CONSIDER
SHARING THE INFLUENCE WITH OTHERS?

- Mention the book in a Facebook post, Twitter update, Pinterest pin, blog post, or Instagram pic.

- Recommend this book to those in your small group, book club, Bible study, workplace, and classes.

- Go to www.facebook.com/MatthewMaher5511, "FOLLOW" and write a review. Or go to www.facebook.com/the-mattmaherstory, "LIKE" the page, and post a comment as to what you enjoyed the most.

- Tweet "I recommend reading #UMAYBTHEONLYBIBLE-SOMEBODYREADS by @mattmaherstory // @5511publishing // #UMAYB

- Pick up a copy for someone you know who would be spiritually challenged and biblically charged by this message.

- Write a review on amazon.com, bn.com, goodreads.com, or cbd.com

PLEASE VISIT US AT
www.5511publishing.com
FOR MORE LITERARY INFLUENCE

FOLLOW THE AUTHOR
ON TWITTER
@mattmaherstory

FOLLOW THE AUTHOR
ON INSTAGRAM
@matthewmaher7

Made in the
USA
Middletown, DE